Hidden History
— of —
EARLY
RICHMOND

D1160775

HIDDEN HISTORY
— *of* —
EARLY
RICHMOND

MAURICE ROBINSON

THE
History
PRESS

Published by The History Press
Charleston, SC
www.historypress.com

Front Cover
Top: Pratt's Castle on Gamble's Hill; Trabue Coat of Arms; Bellona Main Arsenal No. 1.
Bottom: Bellona Cannon at Drewry's Bluff; Painting of Gamble's Hill, 1600s.

First published 2020

Manufactured in the United States

ISBN 9781467143356

Library of Congress Control Number: 2020932086

Notice: The information in this book is true and complete to the best of our knowledge. It is offered without guarantee on the part of the author or The History Press. The author and The History Press disclaim all liability in connection with the use of this book.

"Like a true philosopher, you love the whole human race and are never so happy yourself as when you are administering to the happiness of others."
—1805 letter from John Clarke to William Wirt [1]

To Helen, whose faith and hope in my recovery has gained for her, this day, an everlasting place in heaven.
—Your loving husband, Maurice

Contents

Acknowledgements   9
Introduction   11

1. Richmond's First Huguenot Settlers (1607–1724)   15
2. "Keswick Plantation" Begins the Adventure (1750)   23
3. Secret Foundries: Westham and Bellona (1776–1865)   34
4. Unique Arsenals and Armories:
       Richmond and Bellona (1790–1836)   55
5. What's Hidden on the Seven Hills in Richmond? (1750–1865)   78
6. Silkworm Farm Breeding Worms at Bellona (1837–1842)   120
7. Epilogue: Richmond's Civil War Events (1861–1865)   125

Change of Ownership   145
Conclusion   147
Appendix: Chronological History   149
Notes   157
Bibliography   167
Index   171
About the Author   175

ACKNOWLEDGEMENTS

I t is most important to thank my publisher, The History Press, with which the history of the Richmond, Bellona and Keswick areas of Midlothian and the City of Richmond would not have been recorded in this manner.

I would like to say many thanks to the librarians and officials at the Library of Virginia in Richmond for all their assistance with research and navigating the archives. Without their assistance, I would never have been able to find and write about the unique area of Richmond and Chesterfield.

I also have to give thanks to John Cooki, historian librarian; Cathy Wright, curator from the American Civil War Museum in Richmond; and Matthew Guillen, reference coordinator at the Virginia Museum of History and Culture. I also want to thank Mark Fagerburg, manager of Photo and Digital, and especially Trenton Hizer, senior manuscript acquisitions and digital archivist, who both work at the Virginia Historical Library. And the help of the librarians and archivists at the Virginia State Archives was most appreciated. The Huguenot Society; the Powhatan, Virginia and the Chesterfield Historical Society of Chesterfield, Virginia; the Powhatan County Historical Society; the University of Richmond Library and Archives; the Chester County Public Library; and Joseph Holloway PhD in Porter Ranch, California, also deserve my thanks.

Thank you to everyone at the Chesterfield Historical Society for their assistance in obtaining maps and giving more help than I can remember.

I have great thanks for Banks Smither, my acquisitions editor in New York, for supporting my first two history books and for advising me to place my trust in Kate Jenkins, my acquisitions editor in Charleston, South Carolina, who has done everything to assist me in completing this excellent story.

Special thanks are sent to my brother, Norman Robinson, for all of the proofreading, editing and the many important suggestions he gave to help create this history book and its messages that are informative and enjoyable for all of the readers. And I certainly want to thank Mike Lee for all his expertise in obtaining all of the old pictures that were brought to life in this hidden history.

And I would like to say a final thanks to John Tyler Community College history professors John Kirn and Greg Hansard for their advice and assistance in obtaining vital information from John McClure, the director of library and research; the Virginia Museum of History and Culture; and Kelly Kerney, research assistant at the Valentine Museum. Both of these museums are located in Richmond, Virginia.

INTRODUCTION

This book is a study of how the residents of Powhatan, Chesterfield and Richmond understood the hidden area of their country in the period between 1607 and the Civil War. A major lived and helped develop his home in Powhatan and built armories in Chesterfield and Richmond. In Richmond, the same major helped develop the city and had many different ideas on how to construct the numerous buildings that were needed in Richmond during the 1800s.

In this book, readers will hear about the many ideas that were developed in Richmond and how many of the city's buildings were destroyed during the Civil War. Readers will hear from many Richmond citizens and will learn how they founded, developed and lived on Richmond's Seven Hills during the antebellum period. The stories and histories in this book will explain the area's antebellum period and legacy, and they will bring readers through the Civil War in Richmond and prepare them for living in the period after the war.

Many stories have been written about the unique historical events that occurred on the Seven Hills of Richmond, Virginia, and the areas surrounding them, and I have included them. Each of the Seven Hills in Richmond have unique stories to convey that include significant events before and after the Civil War. I would like to point out that Bellona Arsenal and Keswick Plantation in Chesterfield and Powhatan Counties have a combined story to tell that is also most unique.

So much has been written about the military conflicts that occurred in the city of Richmond during the Civil War and the other conflicts that eventually destroyed many buildings and properties in the city. It seems so unique that all of the stories and histories of the operations in Bellona, which supported these wars, have been forgotten or kept secret for the most part. In this book, I would like to tell the readers the story of how Bellona transitioned from a backwoods operation to a private foundry, adding several governmental arsenal buildings and operating under two flags during two wars. The foundry previously served as a silkworm operation and as a farm with a waterwheel and pigs; today, it is an intimate, luxury community on the James River.

This book will tell readers about the Trabue family, who settled in Powhatan (on the Chesterfield County line) and owned the adjacent Bellona property in Midlothian. Readers will learn about Major Clarke's successes in building the Keswick Home near the Midlothian-Powhatan county line, helping develop the Richmond Armory and Arsenal and participating in developing other buildings in Richmond's downtown area. Readers will learn about how Major Clarke was put in charge of building the Bellona Foundry and, later, the Bellona Arsenal Proper, both in Midlothian, Virginia.

The American Civil War, which began in 1861, brought Bellona and the manufactory back to life in the production of "superior" weapons that were used by the South until the Civil War ended in 1865. After being sold many times, Bellona still carries its historical memories of the many events that took place on this property. Several buildings have been renovated, and some portions of buildings and weapons still exist on the property to remind visitors of its historical past. During the two wars that took place in Bellona's active years, the foundry was never attacked or damaged by the conflicts that took place around Richmond and Chesterfield. This certainly reminds us of how secretive the operations were at Bellona.

The story was quite different for the buildings in Richmond that were damaged or destroyed at the end of the Civil War. Both the Westham Armory and the Virginia Manufactory were gutted by the North at the end of the Civil War. The history of the Virginia Manufactory, which last produced arms in 1821, is confusing because it became the Virginia State Armory and then the Richmond Armory. But it's no secret that the manufactory was destroyed at the end of the Civil War.

On a happier note, I would like to tell readers about the interesting stories about the many unique goings on around Richmond's "Seven Hills" before and after the Civil War. Writing the entire truth about the hidden history of

Richmond is very difficult because I am writing about events that occurred before my lifetime, and many of the buildings mentioned do not exist today. I had to take other's words for the truth. These people normally lived during this period and experienced, firsthand, the events as they happened. However, it was still a privilege for me to attempt, in writing, to place many of the events that happened in and around Richmond, Bellona and Keswick in this historical publication about Virginia.

RICHMOND'S FIRST HUGUENOT SETTLERS

1607–1724

In 1607, when the first English settlers arrived in northern Chesterfield County, they entered the territory of the Monacan Indians, members of the Catawba tribe of the Sioux. At that time, the Monacans were believed to number between eight thousand and ten thousand. Recent archaeological evidence suggests that the Monacans were a significant influence on the decision by the eastern Powhatan Indians to allow the Jamestown colony to survive. The Monacans persuaded the Powhatan Indians to teach the Jamestown colonists how to survive by planting and growing the correct crops, hunting and fishing. The Monacans may have been the Powhatan's chief source for copper, a highly valued commodity. They traded with the Powhatans, mined copper and made necklaces, which Powhatans prized greatly. The Monacans wanted little contact with the English, so the Monacans traded messages through the Powhatans.[2] The early English towns were open settlements rather than the normal palisaded villages, and they depended heavily on agricultural products. The Monacans survived on Virginia's abundant wildlife and then-teeming rivers. In the twentieth century, when the water level was low, the Monacan fishing traps were visible.

In 1687, Antoine Trabue (Trabuc), a French Huguenot who fled Montauban, France, migrated to Virginia. Antoine was born around 1667 in Montauban, Haute-Garonne, Midi-Pyrenee, France, a city on the Tarn River[3] in the province of Cuyenne, a few miles north of Toulouse in southern France. As a young man in his teens, Antoine suffered from religious and civic oppression in France. Many years later, Daniel Trabue, a grandson of Antoine, wrote in his journal:

> *I understood that my grandfather Anthony Trabue had an estate but concluded he would leave it if he possibly could make his escape* [from France]. *He was a young man and he and another young man took a cart and loaded it with wine and went on to sell it to the furthermost guard, and when night came, they left their horses and cart and made their escape to an Inglish* [sic] *ship who took them in. And they went over to Ingland* [sic], *leaving their estates and native country, their relations and every other thing for the sake of Jesus who died for them.*[4]

Again, it was not until 1687 that the Trabues began their family settlement in what is now Powhatan County. The Trabue families were the ones who owned most of the property on the southern border of Powhatan County and the northern border of Chesterfield County along the James River, in what is now Midlothian, Virginia.

Antoine (1667–1724) was married after 1703 to Magdeline, but he was first married to Katherine in 1699 in Holland. Antoine's family name was originally Strabo, but William Byrd changed it to Trabue. Antoine was the son of Guillaume Trabue, a tanner from Montauban. Antoine (Anthony) fled from France in 1687 to escape from France's religious persecution. It was then that Antoine traveled to an area in Virginia called Powhatan. There, he was granted Patent 904 in 1715, which included 163 acres for development, and part of Patent 905, which was issued in 1715 to Jacob Florenoy and was later acquired by the Trabue family. Some of this patented property was situated in Chesterfield County. Many other lands in Virginia were granted to Antoine at later dates.

In England, the Huguenots were treated as temporary refugees, waiting until the policies in France changed again. In the New World, however, the colonies tried to recruit the Huguenots as permanent settlers. Virginia was land-rich and people-poor, and Protestant refugees were prime targets for expanding the local population. It was hard to recruit the Huguenots, but Virginia did have some success. One Huguenot traveler in Virginia in 1686 considered the colony to be too foreign for his taste. Durand de Dauphine fled France rather than recant his beliefs and profess to be a Catholic. While in France, he had already read propaganda from Carolina advertising why it was a good place for settlers. After fleeing to England, Durand de Dauphine determined that he preferred taking a chance, and he examined Charleston in the southern half of the Carolina colony rather than live in exile in the big city of London.

Durand de Dauphine knew he was not the first to choose Carolina over Virginia: "All the French who have gone over have settled in the south." He also knew that the climate in the south was different from France. "It is unhealthy for Frenchmen, which does not surprise me, for the southern provinces of Virginia four degrees further north are also very unhealthy." Murphy's Law certainly applied to Durand de Dauphine's trip; in the end, after nineteen rough weeks of sailing, he finally entered Virginia, passed New Point Comfort and arrived at the North River, which separates Mathews and Gloucester Counties, on September 22, 1686. The idea of settling in Virginia was attractive to the French refugee:

> *The land is so rich and so fertile that when a man has fifty acres of ground, two men-servants, a maid and some cattle, neither he nor his wife do anything but visit among their neighbour. Most of them do not even take the trouble to oversee the work of their slaves, for there is no house, however modest, where there is not what is called a lieutenant, generally a freedman, under whose commands two servants are placed. This lieutenant keeps himself, works and makes his two servants work, and receives one-third of the tobacco, grain, and whatever they have planted, and thus the master has only to take his share of the crops.*

Durand de Dauphine had accumulated capital in France and managed to escape with money. He could have afforded to pay for the passage of an indentured servant, entitling him to fifty acres of land, or purchase land and slaves to work it. He considered the English to be lazy, noting that clothes were imported rather than woven in Virginia, where "not one woman in the whole country [knew] how to spin." He also considered it wasteful to plant without ploughing when the coastal soils were so free of stones. Durand de Dauphine thought the French Huguenots, who were accustomed to working hard to pay Louis XIV's heavy taxes, would thrive in Virginia. "Were I settled there, provided I had two servants, a plough with two cows and another with two horses, I could boast of accomplishing more work than anyone in the country with eight strong slaves."

The Virginia governor, Francis Howard of Effingham, and William Fitzhugh both failed to convince Durand de Dauphine to return to Europe and lead fellow Huguenots back to Virginia. Governor Howard promised to enlarge the standard fifty-acre-per-person land grant (for those who paid their own passage across the Atlantic) to five hundred acres for Durand de Dauphine, but the Frenchman noted:

> *I would have to settle further back and be among the savages, who are not greatly to be feared, but there is some inconvenience owing to the fact that only small boats can sail up the rivers in the back country so one could not trade by water. For this reason, as there are vast tracts of land for sale very cheap, very good and among Christians, he advised me to buy there, rather than further away.*

The governor did promise that the French Protestants could have their own ministers rather than be required to attend Anglican services.

> *And as for the pastors, provided that from time to time they preached in English and baptized and married the other Christians who might be among the French settlers, he would give benefices to two or three, and they would be required to read the book of common prayers when preaching, except when they preached to French people only, they could do as they were accustomed in France.*

In 1699, a Huguenot colony took the Native American land and established a settlement of their own. Through intermarriage with the white settlers or through uniting with other tribes, the Monacan population gradually decreased. Because the river repeatedly overflowed village sites, few traces of native settlements remain in the areas.

FRENCH HUGUENOTS

In 1700–01, between seven hundred and eight hundred French Huguenot religious refugees arrived on five ships from London at Jamestown; they had been promised land grants and settlements in Lower Norfolk County by the English Crown. After claiming that the Norfolk area was unhealthy, William Byrd, a wealthy and influential planter, offered the French refugees ten thousand acres to settle at what became known as Manakin Town, on land that had been abandoned by the Monacans.

Huguenots, the largest single group of French Protestant refugees to come to Virginia, settled near Richmond on the site of a deserted Monacan village in 1700–01. In 1700, the Virginia General Assembly established King William Parish, also known as Huguenot Parish. The Huguenots established a church at this site that is now known as the Manakin Episcopal Church. The first years on the frontier were harsh for the urban French; of the 390 French who settled at Manakin Town, only 150 remained there by 1705. They ran short of supplies and were initially ill-suited to carve an agricultural settlement from the frontier. They did use some land that had been cleared by the Monacans. The French eventually became established and assimilated in colonial Virginia. The services at the Manakin Episcopal Church were gradually held more in English than French. The French ultimately adopted the

Trabue coat of arms, representing the Trabue family in Powhatan and Chesterfield. *Courtesy of www.flickr.com.*

English language and elements of the English culture; they intermarried with many planter families of English descent in the area, and they purchased African slaves as laborers when they could afford them.[5]

In 1700–01, four ships arrived from London within a few months of each other: the *Mary and Ann* (this ship arrived at Jamestown on July 31, 1700, and the passengers proceeded by small boats to land that had recently been vacated by the Monacans); the *Peter and Anthony* (this second ship arrived in Jamestown in September 1700, and the passengers walked to Manakin Town); the *Nassau* (arrived March 5, 1701, and went up the York River); and a fourth ship with a name and passenger list that do not exist today. French Huguenots, having fled religious persecution, had lived in England and Ireland and served in the military for King William. They were granted lands in the New World to build a permanent home where they had the freedom to worship as they pleased.

Peter Jefferson moved his family to Tuckahoe Plantation, across the river from Manakin Town, in 1745, when his son Thomas was two years old. It was Thomas Jefferson who grew up in a world not just of "Old Virginia" families but of second- and third-generation French Huguenot families. One of Jefferson's closest friends at the College of William and Mary, whom he called a "bosom friend," was John Tyler, the grandson of Dr. Lewis Contesse, a prominent Huguenot physician in Williamsburg. (Tyler's grandson became president.) Jefferson had many good friends among the close-knit Huguenot community in Williamsburg. It is said that he helped design the William Pasteur Home (now called the Semple House), which still stands on Francis Street, and he visited there often. Dr. Pasteur, the son of Huguenot immigrant Jean Pasteur, was married to one of Jefferson's cousins, and Jefferson roomed with Pasteur's sister while studying law with George Wythe. Jefferson was also a good friend of Governor Francis Fauquier, the son of a French Huguenot doctor.

So, during his formative years, Thomas Jefferson was close to the children and grandchildren of Huguenot emigrants. One can only speculate as to how his early exposure to French thought and the Huguenot heritage influenced Jefferson's later thinking. Jefferson lived in a relatively small and tight-knit world in Virginia as he grew up. It is always difficult to prove how much one's youthful world influences one's adult thought and philosophy, but there's no doubt that the man Jefferson became was shaped, to some degree, by the religious and intellectual Huguenot heritage of his tutors and close friends.

In 1704, the Virginia House of Burgesses awarded a land grant of ten thousand acres to the French Huguenots from the Colony of Virginia. The grant stated:

> *Resolved, that ten thousand acres of land be laid out at the Manakin Town and appropriated to the use of the French refugees there settled. That every French refugee inhabiting a the Manakin Town and parts adjacent have liberty to take up so much of the said ten thousand acres as will make his quantity of one hundred thirty-three acres.*
> —*Test William Randolph, clerk, House Burgesses*[6]

The first church building in Manakin Town was erected in 1701 on glebe land that had been granted for that purpose. The Huguenots at Manakin Town and in the Colony of Virginia personified piety, ethics, honesty, industry, inventiveness and thrift. They left a mark of rare distinction that greatly enriched colonial Virginia and the nation. Various memorials remind us of these staunch and eminently brave people.

The site of the Huguenot settlement of Antoine was in Manakin Town, just west of Richmond in what is today Powhatan County, Virginia. The first years on the frontier were harsh and difficult. Many of them died in the first year. By 1750, the Huguenots had deserted Manakin Town.[7] The Huguenot Settlement Marker is located on Midlothian Turnpike and reads:

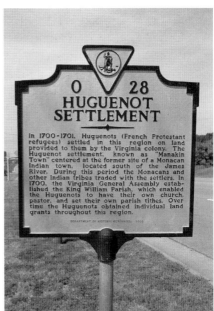

Left: Manakin Town Marker 0-3. Mowhemcho Indian Town was established in 1612 and moved west in 1622, two miles past Huguenot Springs Road. *Courtesy of Powhatan County, photograph courtesy of M. Robinson.*

Right: Huguenot Settlement Marker 0-28. Huguenots settled Powhatan in the 1700s. This is a Virginia State Settlement marker and description that was set up by the Department of Historic Resources in 2000 on Midlothian Turnpike in Midlothian. It is located on Midlothian Turnpike between Murray Olds and Grove Roads. *Courtesy of the Historical Marker Database, photograph courtesy of M. Robinson.*

> *In 1700–1701, Huguenots (French Protestant refugees) settled in this region on land provided to them by the Virginia Colony. The Huguenot settlement, known as "Manakin Town" centered at the former site of a Monacan Indian town, located south of the James River. During this period, the Monacans and other Indian tribes traded with the settlers. In 1700, the Virginia General Assembly established the King William Parish, which enabled the Huguenots to have their own church, pastor, and set their own parish tithes. Over time, the Huguenots obtained individual land grants throughout this region.[8]*

By 1705, many French settlers lived on farms outside Manakin Town in the English manner or had migrated to other parts of Virginia. So, they placed their church and glebe lands in the center of the granted acreage, and that became the center for their farms. The grant was divided more or less equally, with each grantee in 1710 receiving about 133 acres that stretched in narrow lots from the river so that each household would have access to the water. By then, many French families had already migrated to other parts of Virginia and North Carolina. The grants proved to be too limited for growing families. On Trabue's property on the James River, adjacent to Powhatan, the Bellona Arsenal and Foundry was later developed.

"Keswick Plantation"
Begins the Adventure

1750

Early in the eighteenth century, Charles Clarke, a native of Surrey, England, acquired by grant of "more than 1,500 acres" of land that extended south from the James River and lay on both sides of the present boundary of Powhatan and Chesterfield Counties. He married Marianne Salle, a member of one of the original Huguenot families, and around 1732, he established his home around what was later called "the Keswick area" or, earlier, "the Manor House" on the present Powhatan section of his property. Keswick is situated on the south bank of the James River in the northeast corner of Powhatan[9] County, just over the Chesterfield County line, with a small portion of the plantation lapping over into adjacent Chesterfield County.

Again, it was not until 1687 that the Trabues began their family settlement in what is now Powhatan County. The Trabue families owned most of the property on the southern border of Powhatan County and on the northern border of Chesterfield County along the James River in what is now Midlothian, Virginia. The dwelling house at Keswick, which was apparently constructed early in the nineteenth century, is a two-story, gable-roofed, frame-with-weatherboard building. It is supported by brick foundations and has a brick exterior with a chimney on each gable. Each chimney has two sets of stepped weatherings (material used as a weather strip) and a corbelled (brick or stone, slightly extended) cap. All the brickwork is laid in three-course American bond.

The outbuildings at Keswick are to the east and north ends of the house, between it and the river. Beginning with the southeasternmost building and proceeding counterclockwise, Keswick's structures include a well house, a smokehouse, the circular and questionable slave quarters, a kitchen, a two-story brick house, a shed and a laundry. The original residence was known as the "Manor House," and a kitchen and a circular slave quarters building were built close by. These buildings, which were made from brick laid in iron mortar (in this period, iron was used in the mortar for extra strength), are still standing today in

Major John Clarke, son of Charles Clarke, was the owner of Keswick Plantation (1766–1844). *Courtesy of Virginia Cavalcade.*

perfect condition. The questionable slave quarters building has a large central chimney with three fireplaces and shows evidence of having had a second-floor gallery originally with sixteen cubicles.

The Manor House was older than the present Keswick Mansion. This earlier house was probably built by Charles Clarke before John Clarke was born. The Manor House has two stories, with two rooms on each floor. Originally, a solid brick wall separated the first-floor rooms, and each had a separate front door. A staircase on the left side of the room led to the second floor. Parapet walls extended above the roof line, and four courses of bricks were corbeled to form a cornice effect.

It was early in the nineteenth century that Major John Clarke, the probable builder of the main plantation house called Keswick in Powhatan County, constructed the home just on the border with Chesterfield.[10] Earlier, a two-room brick office was built, and after that, perhaps around 1815, a more commodious two-story frame residence was constructed. Different floor levels on the second story suggest that the entire house may not have been built at one time. The residence has a unique H-shaped floor plan that corresponds to that of Tuckahoe, another Colonial-era plantation across the James River in Goochland County that had been built almost seventy years earlier. Inside the home, the front of the first floor consists of one large room, with fireplaces at either end. The mantels are identical, with large, carved rising sun medallions. One end of the room, set off by an arch that is also decorated with the rising sun carving, is fully paneled and may be separated from the balance of the room by folding doors.

Above: Keswick Plantation Home, the home of Major John Clarke, was built in the early 1800s in Powhatan County on its border with Chesterfield. *Courtesy of Wikimedia.*

Left: An aerial view of Keswick Plantation Home on the Powhatan-Chesterfield line, 2018. *Courtesy of the Chesterfield Historical Society.*

The Keswick grounds contain a magnificent grove of a variety of Native American trees and large boxwoods. On the edge of the yard, there is a small family cemetery that contains the graves of Major John Clarke and his granddaughter, Rosebella Burfoot. Major Clarke was born in 1776 as the son of Colonel James Clarke and the grandson of immigrant Charles Clarke. He married Elizabeth Hack Moseley (1776–1806) and was a man of many accomplishments and great energy.

There were happy times at Keswick during the ownership of the younger Clarkes. William A. Archer, the grandson of Colonel John, wrote:

> *In my boyhood days, I was told that Keswick was a very gay household, as it was the favorite resort of the young officers from the arsenal. The*

Keswick household, according to my recollection, was made up of Mrs. Lavinia Wooldridge, Miss Polly Clarke, Mrs. William Wooldridge and Mrs. William Archer. The latter was my grandmother, and the mother of Dr. Julius L. Archer, subsequently the owner of Bellona Arsenal.

In addition to operating the plantation, Major Clarke established an iron foundry, which was instrumental in getting the federal government to build Bellona Arsenal on a part of the property. Clarke occupied a prominent place in Richmond, where he was director of the Virginia Manufactory of Arms and built the first penitentiary, a public warehouse and other public buildings.

The main "mansion" was also known many times as "the Big House." After the Clarkes lived in Keswick, the ownership of the home passed through several different families. In 1961, Mr. and Mrs. Cornelius F. Florman acquired it and occupied it as their home. Former owners had done much to restore the buildings, taking great care in maintaining the home's detail and tradition. The present owners have made additional improvements to the residence and other buildings and have completed the restoration of the grounds by replacing the original entrance road and the approach to the residence.[11] Today, Keswick is situated in a unique location, in that the entrance to the property is physically located in the Midlothian area of Chesterfield County, and the Keswick residence itself is physically located in Powhatan County. Clarke built the main clapboard two-story plantation house. A sunrise-sunset motif is the home's unifying theme. Its unusual H-shaped floor plan, again, echoes the floorplan of Tuckahoe, another Colonial-era theme repeated throughout the home's woodwork.[12]

Keswick is an important example of the distinguished group of eighteenth- and nineteenth-century plantations on the James River above Richmond.[13] It is individually significant for its distinctive plantation complex that contains a notable collection of outbuildings, including an enigmatic circular structure with an original function that has not yet been determined. With its varied forms and apparent single building period, the complex has much to teach about the physical layout and social organization of early nineteenth-century plantation life.

The main house is important for both its fine woodwork and its unusual shape. Again, this floorplan was influenced by Tuckahoe, the famous colonial plantation house. The Keswick house stood then as graphic evidence of the regional and temporal unity of the James River society. There are two Huguenot houses on this property. The original "Brick Manor House" is a four-room building with twin front doors. A separate kitchen is shown in the

A side view of the entrance to Keswick Plantation Home. *Courtesy of the Library of Congress.*

background of the accompanying photograph, flanked by the foundation of one slave quarter and the "unique" round building. All of them were built from brick laid in mortar containing iron ore mined from the property.[14]

It would not be unreasonable to suggest that the "Brick Manor House," with its slipshod brickwork, was erected hastily for the accommodation of the family while a new dwelling house, possibly on the site of an earlier one, was built.[15] The other buildings on the property included:

> The kitchen: A one-story brick building laid in three-course American bond with a gabled roof and end chimney. It has one door, six-over-six sash and louvered blinds. Inside, there is a fireplace for cooking. The floor was made from composite of brick with iron filings that made them more durable. The detached kitchen was an important emblem of hardening the social boundaries and the evolving society created by slaveholders that increasingly demanded clearer definitions of status, position and authority.

> The smokehouse: A covered structure with flush boarding. It has a box cornice, high pyramidal roof and a batten door with

Keswick's outbuilding and smokehouse. *Courtesy of the Library of Congress.*

long strap hinges. Virginia smokehouses were commonly square in construction and topped with pyramidal roofs; they served as an index of the region's diet and were perceived as an important symbol of southern identity by all people.

The laundry: A one-story brick building laid in three-course American bond with a hipped roof and a central chimney with corbeled cap. The façade is divided into four bays; the two on the exterior are doors, and the two on the interior are windows with six-over-six sash and louvered blinds.[16]

The circular building: This building is a total mystery. It seems unlikely that a building so close to the house would be used as slave quarters, but there is a strong tradition that says this was its function. More probable, however, is that it was used for some sort of specialized processing that remains undetermined.

After the death of John Clarke in 1844, his three daughters and two grandchildren inherited the property. In the 1870s, John W. Bellamy began buying shares of Keswick from the property's heirs, and in 1884, he was awarded a total of 465 acres of the property through a chancery suit, *Carrington and Bellamy v. Archer et. al.*, in the Circuit Court of Chesterfield County. Bellamy's heirs held the estate until 1930, when it was sold to G.C. Kirkmeyer. Keswick changed hands several more times until it was acquired by its present owners.[17]

The Circular Building

The Keswick Round Building was probably designed by enslaved artisans in the Midlothian area. Enslaved Africans were responsible for the design and construction of both the plantation house and the slave quarters. The prevalence of certain African architectural characteristics, such as steep, sloping hip roofs; central fireplaces; and porches, suggest that elements of African architecture may have been introduced by enslaved builders.

The most prevalent type of secondary dwellings in the county were slave quarters. Generally associated with large farms or plantations, these pre–Civil War constructions continued to be used as servants' quarters after the war. The change in the societal structures following the war resulted in the diminution and, eventually, the obsolescence of this type of building. By the twentieth century, the slaves' and servants' quarters had given way entirely to tenant houses. Despite the abandonment of this building type, many continued to use the remaining buildings of this type for storage or other farm activities, and they are still in good condition today.

Some properties did not provide separate quarters for the slaves; rather, they included a summer house that served dual purposes. This building type provided space on the ground level for the preparation of food and sleeping space for the slaves in the loft. Summer houses were generally larger than the buildings that only provided slave quarters, and they always included a loft space for sleeping and at least one chimney for cooking purposes.[18]

Structures that used African technologies and skills are found in the slave quarters at Keswick Plantation and others. The slave quarters at Keswick, near Midlothian, Virginia, were constructed around 1750 and were made with the African tradition of handmade burnt clay bricks by plantation slaves. The Keswick slave quarters are more African in their architectural structure, content, form and design.

For the most part, early black architects executed conservative classical designs deep in the African architectural tradition. In time, however, black architects tried to make their designs reflect white American cultural values. African American architects attempted to incorporate African architectural designs in the plantations and the many buildings they built, thus creating an African presence. As a design result of this struggle by African Americans to tell their story through architecture, America has been greatly enriched by the African experience in American architecture—their hidden heritage.[19]

Why would these African architects have built round huts and houses? There are many reasons for round huts like the round building at Keswick. Round buildings use less wall, floor and roof materials than rectangular structures to enclose the same square footage; 20 percent less material is used to create the same sized building. This also means that less surface area of the structure is in contact with adverse weather conditions. The acoustics of a round building's curve softens the sounds inside the building. The shape also prevents noise from penetrating the building from the outside. African architects also understood that a round home's quality is measured in its intelligent use of energy, clever space allocation and its powerful and natural movement of air and sound.[20] The center of round houses became sacred, as that is where the fire would be lit. Prayers would be offered around the fire. God is in the center of the community. A circular leadership structure has neither class nor gender; it is made of people who are meeting to take care of each other, suffer together and pray together—men, women, children and even visitors.

Again, why are African huts round? They symbolize equality, togetherness, leadership in God and trust for one another.[21] However, the original function of the circular building is undetermined. Built in three-course American bond, with thirteen-foot-high walls, the structure at Keswick is about thrity-five feet in diameter. Its conical roof is surmounted by a six-foot-high, five-foot-diameter circular chimney. Plain frames and rowlock lintels enclose the door, and the five windows, with their six-over-six, enclose the door and the five windows with their six-over-six sashes. These openings divide the circumference into six regular arcs, and the three fireplaces in the central stack are each directly on axis with a window. Today, the building's floor is dirt, but a brick floor reportedly lined the interior at one time. Scars on the interior walls reveal the former existence of a gallery (an art exhibition room) eight and a half feet from the present floor, and it is claimed in an article written thirty-five years ago that structural evidence of the gallery's division into sixteen compartments could be seen at that time.[22] The pitch

Keswick's round building with questionable usage. *Courtesy of the Library of Congress.*

Keswick's round building has a chimney inside with three fireplaces. *Courtesy of the Library of Congress.*

of the interior is approximately twenty feet, and the bricks in the floor and about a foot up the wall have iron filings that make them more durable.[23]

John Clarke was an agent of change; even though he built additions to his father's original home, traditionally, the other buildings John built were agents of change. He was challenged to think creatively when helping establish many of the buildings in Richmond, including Bellona and his home at Keswick. Keswick shows that, although John Clarke was an innovative designer of industrial buildings, he was content in building his own residence along traditional lines, using well-established models.[24]

In the early days of Richmond, floors more than twelve inches below ground level and top stories with steeply pitched roofs were exempt from taxes. Therefore, Clarke's house was taxed as only a two-level house, even though he had two floors and a half-underground basement. These early years of the eighteenth century were notable in Chesterfield's history because they saw the beginning of an era of permanent construction. During this time, the different counties were called parishes. Parish lines also underwent more changes due to the spread of settlements. At the beginning of the century, Chesterfield was still a part of Varina and Bristol Parishes. Then, the seating of the Huguenots brought about the establishment of the King William Parish, a small part of which overlapped into Chesterfield. Chesterfield's section of the parish was either dormant

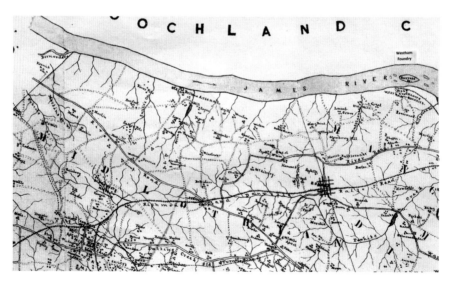

An 1888 LaPrade map that includes the Keswick, Bellona and Westham Foundry areas along the James River. *Courtesy of the Chesterfield Historical Society.*

or became extinct in 1850, when Powhatan was given a slice of the county's area to straighten the boundary line.[25]

It was not until May 25, 1749, that Chesterfield became a separate county after an act of the general assembly to divide the County of Henrico into two distinct counties went into effect. All of the property owned by Chesterfield extended into Powhatan County, but portions along the river were later sold to Powhatan County.

Who first had the idea of constructing a foundry, which had a short life of manufacturing rifles before it was destroyed, on the north side of the James River, near Bellona?

Secret Foundries:
Westham and Bellona

1776–1865

Virginia Foundries and Arsenals

There were about six different foundries located in Virginia during the period before 1865. Since Virginia's coal mining business became so popular, many foundries and arsenals were established in the state. The productive foundries in the Richmond area were: Westham, Tredegar Iron Works, Belle Isle Iron Works, Bellona, Fine Creek, Point of Fork Arsenal, Harpers Ferry and Virginia Manufactory of Arms. Most of these foundries and arsenals were in the business of manufacturing cannons, hand weapons, swords, fences and gates, window protectors, bullets, cannon balls, steam locomotives and ammunitions.

The other main product used to produce steel was coke, which was also very popularly mined and produced in different areas in Virginia. The methods of transportation available were the James River, the Kanawha Canal, the trains and the Chesapeake Bay. All of these transportation routes made it much easier to transport coal to all of the foundries and arsenals.

WESTHAM FOUNDRY

1776–1781

On May 22, 1776, the fifth revolutionary convention approved a proposal to construct a cannon foundry and blast furnace for the manufacture of ordnance. A site at Westham, near Richmond (where Richmond Arsenal was later built in 1798 and, much later, Bellona in 1810), was purchased, and construction began immediately.

Westham Foundry was located across the James River, east of the future Bellona Foundry, which was the closest foundry that was built and functioning before the Richmond and Bellona foundries were in operation. Westham was built at a transportation point on the James River. At the transportation point, the river becomes so rocky that flat-bottom boats have to use the canal to go south or north. It was located at the point where the fall line rocks prevented further river passage. Westham was also established on land that had been owned by William Randolph.

Richmond suffered several British raids in the seven years of the American Revolution, but it was never the scene of protracted fighting or heavy engagements. The town's apparently secure position led the Williamsburg government to store documents there in 1777, and the war accelerated the development of the coal and iron industries near Richmond. The state commissioned the building of a foundry, a boring mill and a magazine known as the Westham Foundry, where coal from Chesterfield's Deep Run pits and iron ore carried downriver from the backcountry were converted into iron and cast into cannons.

After Westham was completed, the foundry complex included eight blast furnaces, a boring mill and the foundry, along with all the buildings necessary to house workers and store supplies. The needs for cannons in the war had initiated this industry at Westham Foundry, which was near the north end of the James River Falls. The Westham foundry was completed in 1779, and in addition to manufacturing civilian tools, it also produced grape canister shot (projectiles in a case) and cannonballs for the Continental army during the Revolutionary War. This, of course, attracted the attention of the British army, which destroyed the foundry in 1781.

But Virginians were most proud of their iron mills. The state's combination of a ready supply of coal from the Midlothian Mines nearby, iron ore barged from the mountains and a steady flow of water guaranteed by the canals assured a healthy iron industry. Not incidentally, there were also numerous black slaves who could do work that most white men disdained, as the tidewater tobacco fields were no longer so fertile.[26]

During the Revolution, both sides made extensive use of artillery. At the beginning of the war, the Patriots had almost no artillery of their own, but Washington used captured British guns from Fort Ticonderoga to drive the British out of Boston in 1776. The Americans eventually developed the capacity to manufacture their own cannons, and they obtained many of the guns they needed from France. High-quality French siege artillery was the key to the great Franco-American victory at Yorktown in 1781. For the Americans, however, the most useful artillery pieces were not heavy siege guns, but lighter pieces that could be moved quickly on field carriages. Mobile field guns traveled with the armies and were used as antipersonnel weapons in battle. Large numbers of light guns also were needed at sea. America sent out hundreds of small privateering vessels, each armed with a few light guns, to prey on British shipping vessels.

During the war, several American iron foundries got into the cannon-making business, not just to support Continental and state military forces but to meet the demands of the privateers as well. One cannon foundry that concentrated on the production of light artillery pieces was, again, Virginia's Westham Foundry. By late 1779, the foundry had begun casting cannons for the Commonwealth of Virginia. Westham produced pounder cannons as well as smaller swivel guns. All of them were cast-iron guns, and none of them weighed more than one thousand pounds. The guns were not just sought for land service with the Virginia forces but also for equipping vessels in Virginia's state navy. The foundry produced ammunition for these guns as well, including cannonballs and grape and canister shot.

The Westham Foundry wasn't unique. Most states had at least one cannon foundry in operation during the Revolutionary War. The foundries certainly didn't produce guns of the same size and quality of the best British and French artillery pieces, and some of these foundries had serious quality control problems. Often, American gun foundries couldn't get the raw materials they needed, and skilled laborers were always in short supply. Nevertheless, these fledgling enterprises went a long way toward meeting America's basic artillery needs during the war, and they made the American forces less dependent on imported tools of war.[27]

The British made a series of devastating incursions into the state that brought Virginia to its knees and forever tarnished Jefferson's reputation. Governor Thomas Jefferson sent arms, military supplies and public records to the Westham Foundry to be stored there. Then Jefferson, his entourage

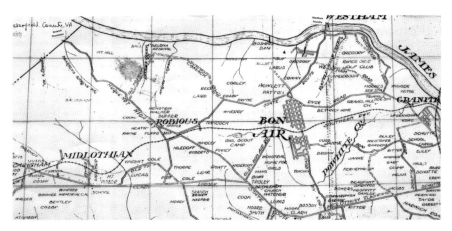

A 1930 LaPrade map of Westham Foundry, Bellona and Keswick. *Courtesy of the Chesterfield Historical Society.*

and many other citizens left the city. The British, unopposed, marched into Richmond, where Lieutenant Colonel John Graves Simcoe of the Queen's Rangers and his troops, on January 5, 1781, continued up the Westham Road to the foundry and destroyed much of the plant's industrial capacity and some of the public records.[28] Simcoe's Rangers then marched back to Richmond, where they found the town almost deserted by the white population. They set fire to public buildings, the ropewalk along the river, warehouses and workshops. When the British forces withdrew—a mere twenty-four hours after they arrived—looters scattered both the county and state records. Although some shots may have been exchanged between local militiamen and the fringes of Arnold's army, the British army met no serious resistance in its brief campaign to Westham. Many slaves departed with the British; British General Clinton had promised freedom to the slaves who would desert the American rebels, but there is evidence that Benedict Arnold and other British commanders considered them booty of war and sold many of those who believed that the British flag meant freedom.

The raid was a signal to Richmond that, after five years, the war had finally moved into Virginia.[29] It was not until after 1790 that the Richmond Armory and Arsenal was built on the city side of the river in downtown Richmond. The entry point of the Kanawha Canal was built in 1790 at Westham, since the rocky portion of the unnavigable river began at Kanawha's entry point. Governor Thomas Jefferson asked for the foundry to be rebuilt, but eventually, the supplies were moved to rebuild the Point of Fork Arsenal in Columbia, Virginia.[30] The arsenal was never rebuilt.

The Virginia Manufactory of Arms was the other major building project during James Wood's governorship. In 1796, the house of delegates passed resolutions for employing additional artificers at the Point of Fork Arsenal and for ascertaining the best location in Richmond for an arsenal and manufactory of arms (December 26, 1796). The period of construction of the aqueduct and canal on the north side of the river correlated with the excavation of the James River Manchester Canal, a continuous navigation canal on the south bank that spanned the distance between Westham at the west end (near present-day Huguenot Bridge) and Broad Rock Island at the east end.

A major proponent of the canal initiative on south side was Major John Clarke, the owner and operator of Bellona Arsenal and the Westham Foundry.[31] Clarke, a manufacturer of military arms and other iron products, had much to gain from reliable and cost-effective water transportation.[32] Even though Westham Foundry was not built by Clarke, he was later intimately involved in the building of the Richmond Foundry in downtown Richmond and Bellona. Clarke's thought was that, later, the south side of the James River was a much safer location for a foundry than Westham. Clarke built his foundry in Chesterfield County twenty-nine years later, in 1810.

It was around the 1810s that Major Clarke established a foundry on the banks of the James River, just upriver from Richmond, Virginia, in Chesterfield County. Some sources indicate 1810 as the official date, while others cite 1816. Regardless, by 1821, the foundry had orders from the U.S. Navy to produce thirty-two- and forty-two-pounder cannons under the Gradual Increase Program after the War of 1812. The declaration of war was passed by the smallest margin ever recorded after a war vote in the United States Congress.

Westham became such a strategic arms center that the British made its destruction a priority during their southern campaign.[33] Westham laid in ruins. The only thing that remained was a brewery, which "was saved by the intercession of the widow who owned part of it."[34] The chance of Westham developing into any semblance of a town was long gone.[35] It was not until 1900 that the Westham Bridge was built across the James River on Route 147, which was opened as a toll bridge, but Henrico and Chesterfield Counties soon bought it and removed the toll in 1920.[36]

Westham's short experience gave Clarke the idea of learning how to specifically develop an armory and arsenal in an out-of-the-way place across the river.

Clark's Bellona Foundry

1814–1865

Because of Clarke's well-established contacts and reputation within the War Department, he was instrumental in obtaining the location of a new federal arsenal at the Bellona artillery production and storage facility. Armories produced firearms, and only two federal government organizations, Springfield and Harpers Ferry, had built them. Arsenals stored, repaired and issued weapons and military equipment in times of need and protected and preserved them when they were not wanted; a much larger number both federal and state arsenals existed.[37]

As the dark clouds of the economy gathered, Chesterfield felt the war's effect on its economy through the launching of new war industries, including the Bellona Foundry and another a power mill. The power mill was connected to one of the nation's earliest commercial tramways, which was built almost twenty years before the first American railway. The foundry was the forerunner of, but distinctly separate from, the Bellona Arsenal, which was established nearby a few years later by the federal government as a belated part of the war effort.[38]

> *Above both cannons from the Lady Dennison are about 5 ft. long and bore diameters are just less than 4" (6 pdrs). The one on the left is possibly Carron design c. 1840–50 very well made much lighter in weight and made of the much stronger malleable cast iron but has no markings on the cannon to indicate it was made between 1815 and 1825 by the Bellona Foundry, Virginia. It is roughly finished—grey cast iron and very heavy. It is marked: 6 3 0 I.C.&Co B.F.V., which stands for John Clarke & Co, Bellona Foundry, Virginia and is of the early making style. The "I" actually stands for J, although why this is so is unknown. The Bellona Foundry was close to Richmond and was a major supplier of cannons to the U.S. and state governments up to the American Civil War.[39]*

The Cannon foundry, which was built before 1810 and before the arsenal, was first located and built about twelve miles west of downtown Richmond, on the south side of the James River. This older establishment, which also bore the name of Bellona, was owned and operated by Major John Clarke of Powhatan County. Clarke (as we have just read) was a man of considerable experience in the manufacture of lethal weapons.

The Bellona cannon on the right is from the *Lady Dennison*, a ship that ran aground at the Wanganui River in 1865. *Courtesy of Geoff Lawson.*

The Bellona Foundry sites lie in the Piedmont Physiographic Province in Chesterfield County, Virginia, on the floodplain and first terrace of the James River.[40]

The casting of cannons was a long and tedious process that involved four basic operations: molding, casting, cooling and finishing. Molding consisted of placing a pattern of the gun to be cast in a box, termed a flask, which was arranged to allow the escape of air and steam. Sand was then rammed around the pattern, which left a cavity into which the melted iron could be poured when removed. When the complete mold was placed together, it was assembled and thoroughly dried. The mold was then placed in a pit and readied for the casting stage. Cannons were made of either iron or bronze (sometimes termed "brass"). Bronze was a mixture of nine parts copper to one part tin. There were no foundries in the South that could cast steel guns. The appropriate metal was melted in a furnace and then poured into the mold, which was filled from the bottom up. As the mold filled, a workman would agitate the liquid metal with a long rod in order to physically bring impurities to the top. Filling the mold took only five to ten minutes.

The entire flask was then removed for the cooling process. Cooling, especially in heavy seacoast guns, created stress and strain, and in an effort to prevent this as much as possible, the flask was surrounded by sand and charcoal. The flask was then left in the pit to cool for three to six days, depending on the size of the casting. Once it was sufficiently cooled, the flask was removed from the pit. Then, a completing team would begin the finishing process. The rough casting was placed in a lathe, and the exterior was turned and finished. The exacting work of boring the interior took several weeks for the tubes of the larger cannon. Following boring, the trunnions were machined to size. Before removal, the exterior was finished and the vent drilled.[41]

In 1810, Major John Clarke and noted Richmond lawyer, William Wirt, established a weapons factory for the U.S. War Department on the south bank of the James River, five miles north of here. Bellona Arsenal (named for the Roman goddess of war) was erected in 1816. After five years of disuse, it was leased to Thomas Mann Randolph in 1837 for use as a silkworm farm. Junius L. Archer bought the property in 1856, and on January 1, 1863, he leased both the arsenal and foundry to the Confederate government. Bellona Arsenal became one of Virginia's leading producers of arms.[42]

As the first superintendent of the Virginia State Armory, Clarke built and managed an arms factory for the fabrication of rifles, muskets, swords and bayonets, and he began the construction of a cannon foundry. Forced out of office in 1809, he decided to turn his talents to the establishment of a foundry of his own. Early in 1814, Clarke and his partner, the eloquent and persuasive William Wirt, the attorney general of the United States, entered a provisional agreement with the army's Ordnance Department to "prepare works and means for the supply of cannon and shot to the United States."[43]

When hostilities became inevitable from the Tredegar Iron Works, Clarke and Wirt received a contract from the government around 1810 and set up a small manufacturing establishment on property that was owned by Clarke on the James River near Spring Creek, where they started turning out cannons, cannon balls, shells and musket balls under the personal supervision of Clarke. To get his products to the nearest shipping point at Manchester, Clarke built a private road to Manchester that became known as the Gun Road. In later years, this road became the River Road and then Old Gun Road. Spring Creek provided sufficient water to drive two water wheels—one for the bellows for the foundry and one to turn the boring equipment in the boring mill. However, additional use of the water to power other machinery via a flume (an artificial channel) arrangement cannot be ruled out.[44]

Confusion exists in both historical records and some modern interpretations in regard to Bellona Foundry and the co-located Bellona Arsenal. Archival investigations have shown that, in a deed from James Clarke[45] to William Wirt that was to be executed in 1814, Clarke sold one undivided moiety (share) in the foundry to Wirt. A forty-foot-wide road to the river was specifically noted along with the Batteau Road Site. The road was undoubtedly used to provide access to the river from the foundry for finished products to be carried up and down the James River.[46] The foundry was a longer distance from the river, and a lake and dam was in the area attempting to get to the river.

> *In twelve acres of land, according to a survey annexed comprehending the said site, including the dam, a road forty feet wide to the river and the ground necessary for the erection of habitations for workmen and the other essential buildings for the convenience of the works reserving to the said John Clarke his heirs and assigns the privilege of erecting as many bridges as he or they may please over the canal through the said land, and a right of road ways over the ground through which the canal passes.*

From that document, the 12.5 acres of land extended south to the current dam across Spring Branch at Reed Pond, which is at the northernmost location possible for a dam, as the valley through which it passes widens very quickly. The property then was evidently designed to be self-sufficient in terms of power needs, as it contained the dam and associated waterways for powering the machinery needed for an iron foundry. It is evident that no such canal was ever constructed, although it was clearly provided for in the agreement.[47]

The War of 1812 demonstrated the immediate need for a weapons factory in the area. The conflict ended in 1814, around the same time that Clarke had begun to build the Bellona Foundry. Bellona originally received a contract to produce cannons and shot for the growing American military during the War of 1812 with Great Britain. A foundry was a separate structure that also required many skilled craftsmen who ate up a higher percentage of profits than a pure furnace operation.[48] Soon after the War of 1812, new orders of coastal artillery were made by the federal government to replace wartime losses and add to the defense of the republic. An agreement was reached

The Bellona cannon resting on an industrial minerals package is from the *Lady Dennison*. *Courtesy of Geoff Lawson.*

with the U.S. Army to "prepare works and means for the supply of cannons and shot to the United States." Within a year, orders were placed.[49] Later, Bellona Foundry became a major weapons supplier that was particularly focused on heavy cannons. The foundry produced twenty-four-, thirty-two-, and forty-two-pounder guns, along with eight- and ten-inch columbiads (Civil War cannons) for army orders.[50] The cannon at Drewry's Bluff has markings that indicate it was made between 1815 and 1825 by the Bellona Foundry. It is roughly finished, made from grey cast-iron and very heavy.[51]

The establishment of a foundry required a steady turnover of product of both iron ore and coal for the final weapons to ensure its success. A little more than a year after the founding of Bellona Foundry, Clarke indicated that he had met the conditions of his agreement, and in March 1813, Clarke and Wirt negotiated a contract to cast three hundred tons of iron cannons for the army. The foundry was an integral part of a major industrial complex that had the primary task of producing armaments for the United States government and for the Confederate government during the Civil War.[52] Bellona Foundry was a major supplier of government ordnance through the antebellum period (period before the American Civil War). Together, with

Left: A Bellona cannon at Drewry's Bluff, guarding the river against northbound attacks. *Courtesy of www. liveandlethike.com.*

Below: A vacant two-story Bellona Foundry building remains near the roadside. *Courtesy of Mark Hunter.*

the Tredegar Iron Works, Bellona gave the Old Dominion two of the five plants that casted heavy cannons on the eve of secession. Although it was outstripped by the Tredegar Iron Works during the war, Bellona served the Confederacy well. Many eight-inch columbiads that were cast at Bellona were appropriated by the Virginia authorities in 1861; the foundry went back into production for the Confederate government in 1862.[53]

Bellona Arsenal was not intended for just manufacturing; it was also meant for the storage of powder, shells and other materials, including muskets that were made in the huge granite mills that had been built along Fine Creek in Powhatan.[54] The army and navy orders for Bellona Foundry dropped off after 1840. The 1840 mix-up with patterns for forty-two-pounders

Huguenot Settlement 0-3. *Courtesy of the Department of Historical Recourses, photograph courtesy of M. Robinson.*

(precision rifle series) may have been a symptom of an underlying problem at the facility. Around the same time, Dr. Junius L. Archer purchased the foundry and, presumably, the old arsenal grounds.

Still, the foundry received only a few token navy contracts. Bellona lagged behind its competitors, such as West Point Foundry, Fort Pitt Foundry and the Boston companies, regarding iron processing and casting techniques. With the advances in metallurgy in the 1840s and 1850s, military contracts called for specific metal composition and smelting practices. Further, the army preferred water-cooled castings (iron for cannons was first extremely hot after it was casted). Bellona (and for that matter, Tredegar, which was farther downriver) was not ready for those practices. In the late 1850s, this changed, as quantity orders from both the navy and army started coming in. As noted earlier, many of those orders were not complete, or at least the weapons were not delivered, at the outbreak of the war.

The combination of Richmond's plentiful coal and its proximity to Bellona Foundry on the James River and to the Tredegar Iron Works hastened the removal of the capital of the Confederacy from Montgomery, Alabama, to Richmond in 1861. The Civil War put pressure on the colliery (coal mine) owners to increase supplies of coal to Confederate munitions factories, such as Bellona Foundry and Arsenal and the Tredegar Iron Works, the most valuable munitions plants in the entire South.[55]

Coal and coke (coke is made by heating coal, which was used mainly in iron ore smelting) began coming in from the Chesterfield and Richmond coalfield in the 1840s, around the same time as the rapid growth in production. For the purpose of satisfying customer needs for its various uses, the uniformity in quality of coal shipments was important. Standards (there were different grades of coal mined in Midlothian) of coal analysis were not set forth until the early 1900s, and methods of collection are unknown. Averages from the following list were not calculated because of the uncertainty of the basis for analysis; that is, they were calculated as received—moisture-free or moisture- and ash-free. It is amazing that there were this many coal mines in Midlothian. Listed below are the coal basins that were located in the Midlothian District:[56]

Location	Reference
Midlothian Pit	Silliman, 1842
Midlothian Pit	Johnson, 1846
Creek Shaft	Johnson, 1846
Black Health Pits	Johnson, 1846
Tippecanoe Shaft	Johnson, 1846
Stonehenge Pits	Taylor, 1855
Maidenhead Pits	Taylor, 1855
Health Pits	Taylor, 1855
Mills and Reid Creed Pits	Taylor, 1855
Wills Shaft	Taylor, 1855
Greenhole Pits	Taylor, 1855
Forbes Pit	Taylor, 1855
Midlothian Pit	Robertson, 1873
Midlothian Pit	Heinrich, 1878
Grove Shaft	Heinrich, 1878
Grove Shaft	d'Invilliers, 1904
Midlothian Pit	d'Invilliers, 1904
Grove Shaft	Wortham, 1916
Murphy Slope	Treadwell, 1928
Morgan Shaft	Eby and Campbell, 1944
Midlothian Pit	Jenny, 1949

The following mine names have been mentioned in literature that reference the Midlothian Mining District, but their locations have not been determined.[57]

Bellona Arsenal Shafts
Bolling (or Boiling) Pit
Diamond Hill Pit
Forbes Pit
Garden Wall Pit
Hill's Pits
Jack Pit Shaft
Rise Shaft

Bellona, much like Tredegar, then became a major supplier for the Confederacy. And as with other prewar efforts, Bellona focused on heavy artillery—columbiads, naval guns and siege guns.[58] Under both Bellona and Tredegar owners, the Bellona Foundry was a major supplier of weapons for the federal and state governments. The initials "B.F." can be found coupled with those of Clark, but on early weapons, "I.C." was written rather than "J.C." in the same manner as those of General John Mason of Columbia Foundry (q.v.). Whether Clark shifted to "J" as Mason did in the 1830s has not been determined. Weapons can be found marked with "I.C. & Co.B.F." and "I.C.B.F." at least until 1830, when "J" was probably substituted for "I." After the foundry was purchased by Archer, the cannons were marked "J.L.A.B.F."[59]

In 1832, after only sixteen years of operation, the arsenal was shut down and its garrison transferred to Fort Monroe at Hampton Roads. In 1835, the *Gazetteer of Virginia* cites several reasons for this move. First, there was the "continuous expense and inconvenience of transportation to and from the arsenal." Another factor was the difficulty the arsenal had in retaining civilian mechanics because of its isolated location. Finally, there was a chronic fear of assault by an organized "band of slaves" from the nearby coal mines, where "a greater number of negroes could be collected in a few hours than any other place in the Commonwealth."

> *Although the latter consideration may seem a pusillanimous reason to abandon a military arsenal, it should be remembered that Nat Turner's rebellion of the previous year had resulted in the deaths of 57 whites, compounding an almost irrational fear of long standing among whites. A generation earlier, Gabriel's Rebellion, whose objective was to kidnap the governor and burn the City of Richmond, failed only because of a last-minute warning and a furious storm that knocked out bridges and communication.*[60]

After Gabriel's Rebellion in 1800, the possibility of organized slave revolts was taken seriously, and the idea of a band of renegade slaves falling on a store of weapons and ammunition was a nightmare too terrifying to be ignored.[61]

Even after the arsenal was phased out of existence in the 1830s, Bellona Foundry continued to turn out cannons, shot, swords and firearms. The foundry also produced such civilian goods as cast-iron railings until the 1860s.[62] Many of these cast-iron railings can be seen today on the front of many of the older homes in Richmond.

A replica of a Bellona Cannon at Drewry's Bluff, guarding the river against southbound attacks. *Photograph courtesy of M. Robinson.*

But problems plagued the Bellona Foundry. In 1863, a fire seriously damaged a large portion of the foundry. The government turned to the Tredegar works to re-equip Bellona, but Anderson at Tredegar vigorously advised against it. He argued that there were insufficient raw materials to keep operating at full capacity. Anderson was overruled, however, and reconstruction started. In June, the government impressed a large lathe that had been recently purchased by Tredegar in Raleigh, North Carolina, and much to the distaste of Anderson, the machine was diverted to Bellona.[63] The Tredegar Iron Works operated throughout the war on a contractual basis in support of the Confederate armory, the navy yard and a number of large private businesses, such as the railroads.

Like other war-related enterprises, the Tredegar Iron Works was scheduled for destruction before the federal army took the city, but General Anderson wanted to preserve it. The Tredegar Works, notwithstanding the serious fire in 1863, had expanded and even modernized during the war, unlike most Southern industries. Before the Yankees entered the city, General Anderson armed his workers and prevented both the authorities and the mob from setting fire to the arsenal. His was the only business south of Main Street to survive the fire, and luckily so because the South

A lunette window on the front of the state capitol building at the end of the Civil War, 1865. *Courtesy of the Library of Virginia.*

needed the Tredegar to rebuild its economy. By August 1865, it was turning out rails to rebuild the South's railroads.[64]

Production was apparently not halted for long at Bellona because of the supply of coke. In June 1865, a Richmond correspondent reported, "The ten-inch columbiads now being manufactured at the Bellona Arsenal, near this city, are said to be equal to any manufactured in this country. These works have been turning out guns from the commencement of the war to the present and not the first one has proved defective in any respect."[65] Then, in February 1864, federal raiders passed nearby. In a panic, workers tossed several unfinished guns into the James River; one of them, with a casting flask, was recovered during the Civil War's centennial year. The unfinished gun was likely intended to be a thirty-inch rifle and indicates

Bellona Arsenal 1950

Above: A Bellona Foundry cannon that was relocated to Drewry's Bluff. *Courtesy of the Library of Congress.*

Left: A close-up picture of the remaining two-story Bellona Foundry building in 1950. *Courtesy of the Library of Virginia.*

Bellona produced at least some field guns during its day. The gun and flask stand today as reminders of Bellona Foundry along an aptly named Old Gun Road in a residential area of Chesterfield County, Virginia.[66]

Today, only one building that may have been used in the actual production of cast iron still stands at the site. A structure made from three-course American bond brick stands in a level field beside the foundations of two other brick structures. A few yards north, set into the side of a steep hill, there is a two-story, one-room building that has recently lost its roof. Possibly erected as an overseer's dwelling and office or a workshop, it can be entered at ground level on both floors; there is a door at the second story on the uphill side and a "basement" entry on the opposite façade at the bottom of the slope. Farther up the hill, there is a mid-nineteenth century frame barn with unusual false plate construction. (Flat or titled false plates are used to steady the joists at the bottom of the roof rafters.) Nearby, mounted on a masonry pedestal, there is a large iron cannon that was recovered from the James River on August 18, 1962, by C. Merle Luck, the then-owner of Bellona Arsenal; the cannon was put in the river during Dahlgren's raid during the Civil War.[67]

With the success of Clarke's own foundry, why would he want to name his place of success Bellona? The Bellona Foundry area consisted of many different sites that have since been identified for the many activities in the production of the finished product. A few of them are labeled as follows: the boring mill, the cabin site, the batteau road site, the mound site, the yak pasture site, power source, millrace, office, bellona smithy four areas, flask and gun, brick clay pit, reeds pond, dry pond, kiln, boring mill and the bellona furnaces.[68] The mound site, which measures approximately twenty-five feet square, is now interpreted as the brick kiln. The mound was interpreted to be the remnant of a brick kiln that supplied brick to Bellona Foundry, as it was, without a doubt, included in the original Clarke holdings purchases specifically for the foundry operations. The bricks were clearly handmade, indicating a construction date prior to the second half of the nineteenth century. Bricks were a constant need for an iron works due to the intense heat generated by the process. The heat "ate away" the brick lining of the foundry and required relatively frequent maintenance.[69]

The yak pasture site revealed that the structure's materials, which were initially described as a layer of slag and iron objects at the base of an approximately one-foot-thick plow zone, were in fact shown to be discrete spatially from the mound and were separated from the mound by at least one hundred feet. The dry pond was the source of raw materials, and the bricks were fired at the mound site. Reed Pond provided the water to power the earliest manifestation of Bellona Foundry. Spring Creek, or Sassons Creek as it appears in some nineteenth-century deeds, outlets today from Reed Pond via a modern concrete spillway.

A millrace (channel of water) was dug from Reed Pond to the Foundry; this feature is approximately twenty to thirty feet wide and up to ten feet deep. The terminus of the millrace is opposite the intersection of Old Gun Road and the Batteau Road. The Bellona office structure is located north of Old Gun Road, elevated slightly from the floodplain. The source of the clay for the Bellona brick clay pit and the brick kiln appears to have been the now dry pond, which is currently in the floodplain of the James River on Spring Creek.[70]

The foundry's northern boundary was at the river bank; it was of course fixed, as was the original boundary with the Bellona Arsenal. The southern boundary was agreed upon as the beginning of the headrace (a channel leading to the water wheel) of Reed's Pond, which supplied water to the foundry.

Ironworking Sites[71]

Bellona Power Source
Reed Pond
Bellona Millrace
Millrace and Sluicegates
Boring Mill
Iron and Munitions
Foundry
Batteau Road
Road from River to Bellona Foundry
Bellona Kiln and Brickyard
Brick Kiln
Yak Pasture
Artifact Scatter
Bellona Clay Pit
Dry Pond
Bellona Cabins
Domestic Structures

Above: A view of the Bellona Keswick Plantation Home. *Courtesy of the Chesterfield Historical Society.*

Right: Confederate lab explosion on Browns Island, at SA 101, the entrance to the island. *Photograph courtesy of M. Robinson.*

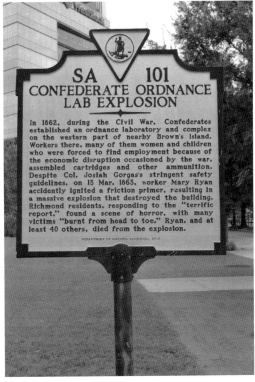

SA 101
CONFEDERATE ORDNANCE
LAB EXPLOSION

In 1862, during the Civil War, Confederates established an ordnance laboratory and complex on the western part of nearby Brown's Island. Workers there, many of them women and children who were forced to find employment because of the economic disruption occasioned by the war, assembled cartridges and other ammunition. Despite Col. Josiah Gorgas's stringent safety guidelines, on 13 Mar. 1863, worker Mary Ryan accidently ignited a friction primer, resulting in a massive explosion that destroyed the building. Richmond residents, responding to the "terrific report," found a scene of horror, with many victims "burnt from head to toe." Ryan, and at least 40 others, died from the explosion.

DEPARTMENT OF HISTORIC RESOURCES, 2002

As Clarke appears to have been a proficient ironmaster, his operational layout may have proven instructional in comparison with others. If craft specialization in the eighteenth century led to a development of industry, as it is currently conceived in the early nineteenth century, then the layout of the structure may have provided clues to Clark's view of efficiency of production.[72]

Production figures for the Bellona Foundry are currently virtually unknown. Spotty records exist for cannon production, but the amount of raw material going through the foundry within a given year are unknown. It is assumed that, at its simplest, the James River provided much of the transportation from upstream for raw materials. The foundry was dependent on raw materials in the form of pig iron.[73] The number of guns that were later cast (at Bellona) for the Confederate government is purely conjectural. However, from all available sources, it can be determined that Bellona cast around 135 heavy guns for the Confederate government—second only to the Tredegar Iron Works.

Unique Arsenals and Armories:
Richmond and Bellona

1790–1836

In the late 1700s, the Virginia Manufactory of Arms was just a thought of the then-governor of Virginia. Virginia governor John Woods selected thirty-one-year-old John Clarke of Powhatan County as his man, as he was well known and respected as a successful millwright.

Clarke selected a parcel of land that was just over six acres in size and located just outside the city limits of Richmond; the land was bordered by the James River to the south and the James River Canal to the north. The land sloped from the higher canal side of the property, down to the James River. The topography of this land parcel allowed for several waterfalls, thereby permitting reuse of the same water three times before it reached the lower river. The land was ideal for minimizing water usage and producing bricks, and its location outside the city limits protected the city and its inhabitants from fires that may have broken out in either the armory or the city. The parcel was also located next to the state penitentiary, a source of needed labor. Virginia paid a total of £550 ($2,667) for the land—a huge sum in 1798.

Clarke traveled to the Springfield, Massachusetts Armory in the north to locate ideas on the layout of the armory. He borrowed many ideas, methods of bookkeeping and manufacturing designs from the Springfield Armory. In 1798, Clarke drew up his plans, which were approved in 1799. By the summer of 1799, construction began on the Bellona Armory. Virginia's governor James Monroe wanted to be able to produce 4,000 stands of arms per year. "The buildings formed a rectangle, all of brick (but one)

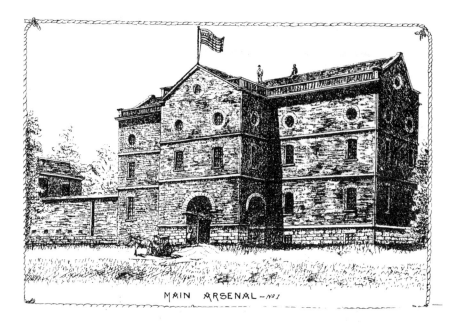

MAIN ARSENAL—N°1

Bellona Main Arsenal No. 1, a three-story building with walls three feet thick that was built in 1816 on the James River. *Courtesy of Gaines, 1953.*

with a stone foundation. The outer walls were without windows—only gun ports."[74] As planned, at full capacity, Clarke's designs for the armory could employ 150 workmen, who would manufacture 4,992 stands of arms annually (16 per day x 312 labor days). In 1801, with construction of the Virginia Manufactory nearing completion, Clarke again traveled north to locate trained, experienced workers.

It was in 1702 that coal was discovered in the Midlothian area of Chesterfield County, but it took forty-eight years before coal was, physically and commercially, produced. Close to Midlothian were the old Trabue coal pits, which extended to the James River, near Bellona Arsenal. These pits were owned by Thomas M. Burfoot and were under lease to Standford Duval and Company. The inferior quality coal from these mines was mainly sold for domestic fuel.[75]

Clarke looked to hire specialized laborers, as opposed to one worker who would make all parts for the production of an entire weapon. Thus, the start of industrial specialization that he observed during his tour at the Springfield Arsenal began his implementation of the new procedure. David Ames from the Springfield Arsenal did not want Clarke to visit any

A drawing of the Bellona Arsenal Farm. *Courtesy of Timmons 1922 map.*

other arsenals, as a number of his trained artificers decided they wanted to go to Richmond and work for John Clarke.

The portions of the manufactory designed to produce cannons, including the large foundry, were not completed until early January 1809. The total expenses incurred to erect the armory amounted to $164,210.55. Later constructions during the Civil War included two small cannon houses and a circular one-story powder magazine; both were built within the courtyard. The original architectural plans of the Virginia Manufactory of Arms have not yet been located and may be lost forever. There are existing records from the armory, and they are located in the Library of Virginia.

By 1820, the federal government was not able to produce the required number of arms for its states because of budget cuts, so the Virginia Manufactory outgrew its reason for existence. The Virginia Manufactory existed from 1802 to 1821; its name changed to Virginia State Armory in 1821, and the name changed again to Richmond Armory or Richmond Arsenal in 1861. The building was destroyed in 1865, at the end of the Civil War. The building was next to the Tredegar Iron Works in 1802. The arsenal was transferred to the CSA in June 1861, and by October 1861, it was producing Richmond Rifles. Each CSA arsenal had an associated manufacturing facility, and in the case of the Richmond Arsenal, the major supplier was the Tredegar Iron Works next door.[76]

At the outset of the war, the arsenal commander of the Frankford, Pennsylvania Arsenal, Captain Josiah Gorgas from the Ordnance Department, resigned his commission on March 21, 1861, and fled to Confederate Richmond with a significant supply of federal rifles and ammunition. Gorgas, who had served in every U.S. arsenal, became the chief of ordnance for the Confederacy, with the rank of major, and was ultimately promoted to brigadier general. His tenacity and ingenuity kept the CSA arsenal system, and specifically Richmond Arsenal, operating throughout

Edward Beyer's sketch of the Virginia Manufactory of Arms ca. 1840.

The Manufactory of Arms in the City of Richmond after it was destroyed at the end of the Civil War. *Courtesy of Wikimedia.*

the war. He created the CSA arms industry from scratch in short order with two of the major arsenals, Bellona Arsenal and Richmond Arsenal.

Each CSA arsenal had an associated manufacturing facility, and in the case of the Richmond Arsenal, the major supplier was the Tredegar Iron Works next door.[77]

VIRGINIA MANUFACTORY OF ARMS

1802–1821 (Virginia's Armory and Richmond Arsenal)

Virginia was the first state to become fully aware of the need to arm its citizenry. Such awareness predated 1800 and showed a foresightedness far ahead of its time. It was another fifty years before South Carolina followed suit.

The Virginia Manufactory of Arms was at the base of Gamble's Hill, which covered over six acres. Established in 1798 by the Virginia General Assembly as a state-owned armory and arsenal, Virginia's Manufactory of Arms produced muskets, rifles, pistols, swords and cannons for the state's militia between 1802 and 1821.

Given the pivotal role that small arms manufacture played in the growth of manufacturing techniques in the nineteenth century, data derived from research at the Virginia Armory site points to its great importance. The Richmond Armory, together with the adjacent Tredegar Iron Works and the Confederate Laboratory that was located to the south of the armory on Brown's Island, reportedly produced nearly half of the armaments and munitions used by the Confederate forces.[78]

Reasons for Virginia's Armory

A defenseless state invites to insult and invasion,
and no situation is so much so as that of a people unarmed.
—Governor James Monroe, 1802

Virginia was proud of its heritage and its possibility of being the only state in the country to operate its own armory to arm its people. Virginia had been closely associated with arms manufacturing; Westham Foundry on the James River, near the thriving city of Richmond, undertook the production of badly needed cannons and ammunition.

Virginia soon realized that contract arms were not the solution to the problem of obtaining suitable weapons. For the five-year period between 1797 and 1802, the state had managed to acquire, on average, approximately 2,680 muskets annually. The numerous frustrations involved with even this small number gave even more impetus for the construction of a state armory.

The Beginning

And to ensure a supply [of arms], *be it further enacted that the executive be empowered*
to establish a manufactory of arms within the vicinity of Richmond, at such place, and
upon such terms and conditions as to them shall seem expedient.
—Shepherd's Statutes at Large

The mammoth task that laid ahead required the special and selected skills of an architect, an engineer, an artist, a diplomat and a businessman. The diversity of personality, as well as the ability required to execute such an assignment, clearly called for a highly gifted man. By whatever methods employed, the executive ultimately chose John Clarke of Powhatan County. It was executed by Mr. Clarke, who was known to be extremely well-skilled in the erection of works of every denomination. Clarke tentatively selected the tract of land in Richmond on the canal and James River.

The proposed site was located near the penitentiary, where additional labor could be procured. Even though they knew that there could be a lot of disease and death among the inmates, which could have been brought on by the miamas, an infectious disease of the river, any health problems that could have arisen were overlooked. Clark's proposal was accepted.

THE EARLY STAGES

I, with pleasure, embarked in the business assigned me by the executive, not without regretting that altho' nature has furnished the United States with the most profuse abundance of materials proper for the fabrication of every species of arms, yet none of our sister states have fallen upon the plan, or followed the example of Virginia, in establishing within themselves the means of protection.
—John Clarke, 1801

The construction of the manufactory began in the late 1700s. Toward the end of 1800, Clarke wrote Governor Monroe that the masonry executed on the east wing was little better than the work that had previously been done on the west wing, as the walls were so weak in places that it was necessary to support them with additional stonework, and in some places, the masonry had crumbled, further weakening the structures. With executive approval, Clarke directed to add stone abutments to the walls for support. This was one of many problems that Clarke encountered.

We have examined the old buildings, fixtures and waterpower of the present Armory at Richmond, the location, arrangement, waterpower and

Bellona half plaque, currently inside the Bellona home, over the fireplace. *Courtesy of the Library of Virginia.*

buildings are far beyond anything we had anticipated. The buildings are amply sufficient for all practical purposes. The walls are very strong and durable—they are arranged as they should be....The waterpower here is infinitely superior to that at Harpers Ferry or Springfield Armory.

There is a possibility that the original plans for the foundry were also altered somewhat, although exactly what these changes were has not yet been identified. However, the two buildings must have been near completion by April 1808, when Clarke requested additional information concerning setting up the machinery. The construction of the foundry and boring mill was finally completed in 1809; this made the Virginia Manufactory of Arms ready for proving on June 30, 1809.

A GLANCE AT THE NEW INSTITUTION

The Armory is constructed for making all the implements of war; and when the foundry for ordnance shall have been completed; every species of arms may be manufactured therein.
—John Clarke, 1804

The main section of the armory contained twelve rooms, and it had three offices on the first floor. On the first floor, there was a guardroom, various storage rooms and the kitchens. The second floor served as living quarters for the workmen and as storage. There was a 588-pound armory bell that was used so that the artificers, who may have, on occasion, found themselves in remote sections of the city, could hear it and distinguish the sound from the smaller bells of the state capitol and penitentiary. A forebay, or collecting pool, was located in each wing, and the water from these reservoirs was used as needed by releasing it to flow over the waterwheels, thereby supplying the necessary power to operate the machinery. The second floor of the eastern wing was used primarily as an arsenal. Clarke engineered the construction of the armory to meet all of the aspects of manufacturing arms.

TOOLS AND MATERIALS FOR THE ARMORY

As I viewed the works and machinery, I will not hesitate to say that they display a comprehensive mind in the arrangement and plan of the whole, and on ingenuity and skill in the execution well regulated by a knowledge of mechanical principles.
—Governor John Pope, 1803

Fire was always a persistent danger to the institutions because of the nature of the operations that were carried on within the building. The main building had been designed with a cupola on each wing to hold water in case of fire. The first armory fire broke out in April 1803. Because of this near disaster, Clarke was authorized to purchase an engine and sixty buckets from Philadelphia. A second fire broke out at the armory in July 1824. The fire was extinguished with little damage. But the last fire on April 3, 1865, destroyed the building.

MUSKETS

The primary objective of the Virginia Manufactory of Arms was to manufacture muskets for the state's infantry. The first thirty-eight Virginia Manufactory muskets were completed in October 1802 by George Charter and Joel Horton. By the end of the armory's first production year, approximately 336 muskets, complete with bayonets, had been finished. The future muskets were made on a compromise, using the best features of each feature on the muskets made at the two federal armories (Springfield and Harpers Ferry Armories), which was recognized by Clarke.[79]

On the night of April 2, the Richmond Armory was gutted by the evacuation fire that swept through the munition. The remains of the Virginia Manufactory of Arms retained architectural and technical information about the earliest phase of industrialism in the United States and information concerning modifications for the technically advanced machinery of the Civil War Period. The manufactory also retained prior modifications as it attempted to regain its former prominence as an iron works.

JOHN CLARKE'S RICHMOND CONTRIBUTIONS

The majority of correspondence in James Monroe's executive papers originates from the Virginia state government. Significant correspondents from the Virginia state government include John Clarke, the superintendent of public buildings. Two significant building projects that were started by Governor James Wood continued during Monroe's governorship with work on the penitentiary and manufactory of arms. John Clark, the superintendent of those two building projects, corresponded frequently with the governor.

John Clarke also devoted substantial correspondence to the construction, employment and materials of manufactory of arms. Clarke wrote Monroe about a trip north to locate artificers to work in the manufactory. In Clarke's absence, Monroe named William McKim as supervisor. Subsequently, on June 12, 1801, Clarke wrote about the number of workmen who were to be employed in the manufactory and the manner in which he proposed to conduct them. Clarke also wrote about the precise number of master armorers, clerks, commissaries and machinists that were necessary for the manufactory. On December 23, 1801, Clarke wrote to the governor defending his conduct as the superintendent of the manufactory following an inquiry of the general assembly. On January 4, 1802, Clarke enclosed an estimate of the expense in the completion of the manufactory of arms and the penitentiary and for the purchase of tools. Lastly, on August 21, 1802, Clarke informed the governor of the death of George Prosser, who served as assistant superintendent for the erection of public buildings.

Additional Clarke letter subjects included: the roofs of the manufactory buildings (April 18, 1800), proposal by George Williamson to repair old arms at the penitentiary (October 1800), arms sent to the penitentiary (January 7, 1801), bells for the manufactory, penitentiary and capital building (April 27, May 2 and February 25, 1802), apprentices to work on the manufactory (April 10, 1802) and the kitchens of the manufactory (November 7, 1802).

John Clarke was also involved in miscellaneous projects, including a project to construct a new tobacco warehouse along the James River Canal in Richmond. On March 28, 1801, Clarke enclosed proposals to the governor for the tobacco warehouse. Shortly thereafter, he submitted proposals for building the walls (June 13, 1801). On July 24, 1802, Clarke wrote the governor concerning the posts for the warehouse. He also wrote about the purchase of slate from either New York or Philadelphia (September 18 and November 8, 1802).[80]

CLARKE'S LUNETTE WINDOWS AT THE CAPITOL

In 1801, Clarke was intimately involved in some of the changes that were made to the state capitol in Richmond. As originally envisioned by Mr. Jefferson, in its early years, the capitol had no windows in the south pediment. In a letter dated January 27, 1801, Clarke suggested that the garret of the capitol could be adapted to store muskets if some modifications were made. Clarke's thought was that the garret was a safe, out-of-the-way location and that a southern lunette window could keep the muskets dry. The lunette in the garret, suggested by John Clarke, was added to the south pediment but not to the north one. Clarke also recommended that additional lightning rods be installed on the capitol's roof.[81] This would prevent fires from being started by lightning strikes.

Clarke was made the superintendent of the armory by Governor James Monroe in 1802 with a salary of $2,000 a year. When he was in charge of building the armory, he received a similar salary; however, the positions were somewhat different. As the superintendent of the armory, he had to supervise the entire building, as well as the artificers who were employed, and attend to all the business of installation. In March 1803, Clarke was made major commandant of the Independent Corps of Artificers. Although there was an attempt to organize the artificers into a military unit, the workers considered themselves gunsmiths, and the military organization of the armory was never fully realized. Nonetheless, it was proper for people to speak of Clarke as a major, and he used this title.[82]

Sometime in 1809, Major Clarke became involved in political troubles. Evidently, muskets for the state militia were being stored in the state capitol's attic, and some additional light was welcome. This simple window appears in paintings of the building in the 1830s. By 1858, it appeared that the original rectangular window had been enlarged to include a fan or arch design at the top. Around 1862, during the Civil War, two additional windows were created in the shape of a quarter-circle on either side of the central window. This was done, apparently, to improve the lighting in the storage area over the portico. The arrival of the Confederate congress created space shortages in the capitol, requiring the state library to move many of its books into portico storage. The librarian made favorable mention of the windows in his annual report. The three fanlight windows remained in the portico until the capitol was renovated and expanded between 1904 and 1906. The pediment windows were entirely removed, and the pediment was restored to its original appearance during the restoration, when the roof and pediments were rebuilt.[83]

The architect who planned those renovations was John K. Peebles, a graduate of the University of Virginia who had a degree in engineering. Peebles was in tune with Jefferson's original architectural vision and intentions for the capitol. Accordingly, he removed the windows from the portico so that it would more closely conform to Jefferson's original vision of a classical temple. Photographs that show the north pediment on the capitol in 1865 show one small rectangular window, which may have been the result of Clarke's original recommendation from 1801. The north pediment does not seem to have had the same evolution of larger and more numerous windows over time as the south (front) pediment over the portico did.[84]

The original lunette in the capitol's pediment had a fan-shaped design and was not set as a rectangular frame. After 1858 and before 1865, two side windows that resembled half fans were added, and the original lunette was extended down to the base of the pediment with a section of square panes, presumably to admit more sunlight.[85]

RICHMOND ARMORY AND ARSENAL

As the owner of Keswick Plantation, Clarke had gained experience in hiring and working with builders, laborers and contractors, assessing the quality of local building materials and managing slaves. He could also estimate expenses and amounts of needed materials, and he could design functional buildings as they were needed.

As with any other plantation, slaves carried out most of the work on-site, with a handful of white workers acing as overseers. Slaves occupied an increasing number of skilled positions as the years progressed.[86] This trend was mirrored at nearly every Virginia iron plantation.

Clarke knew how the infrastructure in Richmond and Virginia society worked. The Commonwealth of Virginia relied on John Clarke's advice and architectural expertise. The Virginia government was much more comfortable and familiar with dealing with someone like John Clarke.[87] Clarke had more architectural expertise and other infrastructure knowledge than anyone else who could be hired or who was available at this time.

VIRGINIA MANUFACTORY OF ARMS

1798

Virginia appropriated funds in January 1860 to modernize the Virginia Manufactory with arms-making machinery that had been manufactured in England, but the confrontation at Fort Sumter initiated the Union blockade, which prevented the machinery from being delivered. In 1861, the Confederacy captured the Union-held town of Harper's Ferry in western Virginia and salvaged the machinery there that was used to manufacture Springfield Model 1855 muskets. The machinery was shipped on the *Winchester* to Winchester, Virginia, where it was transferred by wagons over the Valley Pike to be reloaded onto the Manassas Gap Railroad at Strasburg, Virginia, for delivery to Richmond.

The Old State Armory building with Harpers Ferry Machinery was transferred to the control of the Confederate States in June 1861. The production of Richmond rifles began in October 1861 and continued until the supply of wooden stocks was exhausted in January 1865. A majority of the facility was destroyed during the evacuation fire of 1865. The rolling mills survived the destruction and became part of the Tredegar Iron Works after the war. Portions of the main arsenal building survived in ruins into the late nineteenth century, until it was finally demolished in 1900.[88]

The selection of John Clarke as director of the new armory is as unclear to historians today as it was then. But Clarke was chosen and began a survey of land suitable for the armory along the James River.[89] Major John Clarke was appointed superintendent of the Richmond Armory in 1798. Clarke visited the armory in Springfield, Massachusetts, and the Cecil Iron Works in Maryland. He wrote the governor about his trip on March 7, 1798, from Philadelphia. He wrote again on March 10 concerning his failure to have four thousand weapons manufactured in Philadelphia, and he considered the possibility of having arms imported from France. On April 10, 1798, Clarke informed Wood about his delay in reaching Springfield. On July 23, 1798, Clarke remarked on the cost of the houses, waterworks, et cetera for the manufactory of small arms. Shortly thereafter, he commented on the cost of stonework (July 27, 1798). Lastly, Clarke wrote on several occasions about the digging of the foundation by Moses Bates (November 19, 1798, and March 21, June 15, August 20 and October 19, 1799).[90]

The Virginia Manufactory of Arms was, like the penitentiary, a project far beyond the scope of any building that had been attempted in Richmond,

Bellona Arsenal's adjacent two-story building in the 1900s. It is now the other half of the home. *Courtesy of the Library of Congress.*

Bellona powder magazine's stone wall ruins. *Photograph courtesy of M. Robinson.*

or Virginia as a whole. It was John Clarke's job to choose a site, design the building and its machinery, find artisans to operate the machinery and to make sure that the manufactory did its job of supplying the state with high-quality weapons.[91] Regardless of who made the manufactory drawing for the building, the idea for the design came from John Clarke and demonstrates the range of his diverse abilities and talent.

Clarke was charged with finding and hiring skilled artisans to work at the manufactory and with organizing them as a militia unit. Because Clarke was to oversee the militia unit, he was given the title of major, which he kept; and it is inscribed on his tombstone at Keswick.[92]

THE ARMORY SCANDAL

In January 1808, the general assembly unanimously reelected Major John Clarke as the superintendent of the Virginia Manufactory of Arms, as he had been for the past eight years. But hints of the coming trouble first appeared in the summer of 1807, when Clarke voluntarily submitted to an investigation of the manufactory. The committee reported in January 1808 that some of the arms made before 1806 contained inferior quality iron. The report also mentioned that several weapons made before 1806 had burst when tested by the committee. Clarke's reply to the report was hardly conciliatory; he pointed out that the governors had been continuously aware of the problems involving the supply and quality of iron. Accusations flowed freely from the *Virginian*; the articles, combined with rumors, caused the council of state to initiate a second investigation in June 1808.

It had been obvious for some time that Clarke had enemies in the house of delegates, but the power of his enemies was not apparent until December 9, 1808. On that day, Daniel Sheffey of Wythe County did not mean to avoid another investigation; he intended to take over the proposed investigation himself. Not once during the eight weeks of investigation was Clarke allowed to testify on his own behalf. Not one member of Sheffey's committee personally visited the manufactory during the investigation. The manufactory's payroll records were examined in only two hours, and John Clarke was not allowed to plead his own case. He was dismissed, and the general court was ordered to try him for fraud.

In the face of such treatment, Clarke had no honorable choice but to defend himself in a series of open letters titled "To the People of Virginia," which were published in the *Richmond Enquirer*. The letters set forth his viewpoint quite clearly. Clarke believed strongly that his own "ruin was merely incidental and subordinate to this grand scheme" of undermining the constitution of the state. His efforts were successful. After a weeklong trial, the general court ruled "that the defendant was perfectly innocent of the charge of fraud." Though his name had been cleared, Clarke was unemployed. Soon after the trial, he and William Wirt established the Bellona Foundry on the James River.[93]

BELLONA ARSENAL PROPER IS BUILT

1815–1865

Major Clarke was in Washington on foundry business and possibly arsenal business when he learned that Congress had authorized the construction of new arsenals and that the secretary of war, James Monroe, had decided to locate one of them in Virginia. One might suspect that a kind of logistical law of gravity dictated the eventual choice of the site, but the energetic Clarke did what he could to help the process along, and he was in a position to at least make some very detailed suggestions. To be sure, he sought no pecuniary benefit for himself. Indeed, as he told Lieutenant Colonel George Bomford, who was then the chief of ordnance, he "felt for his country." Nonetheless, he thought that Chesterfield County, where his foundry was situated, would be an excellent place for the arsenal, and he personally knew of several desirable sites in the vicinity of his shops.

After promising to use his influence on the owners, he hurried back to Virginia to open the maneuvers of persuasion. One of the sites that he had mentioned belonged to William Trabue and was located immediately upriver from the foundry. In September 1815, Trabue sold 27.5 acres to the United States. Construction began early that year under the supervision of Robert Leckie, the master mason in the employ of the ordnance department. Trabue's property had come into the possession of Jacob and John James Trabue, the sons of Antoine Trabue, one of the French Huguenots who fled from France in 1687. When Antoine died in 1724, he left his property, which was mostly in Powhatan County, to his sons, and they added the Chesterfield tract to their inheritance. The property conveyed to the government comprised 16.5 acres and cost $4,310. Polly Trabue and Mary Reddy joined in the deed of conveyance.[94]

In 1816, the United States Ordnance Department erected an arsenal in what is now Chesterfield County, Virginia, west of Richmond on the south bank of the James River. The site consisted of 27.5 acres, providing a commanding view of the river valley and the surrounding county. It was acquired from the Clarke family, whose nearby seat was Keswick in today's Powhatan County. Major John Clarke, the grandson of Charles Clarke, who was the owner of Keswick, had previously established an iron foundry on adjoining property.

According to an article in the *Huguenot*, Jacob Amonet, in 1715 and 1716, received two patents from Lieutenant Governor Spotswood for an aggregate of 274 acres "on the south side of the James River in Chesterfield County," and both tracts were parts of the land surveyed for the French refugees. On the first tract, Amonet built an imposing brick residence for himself, which was named Bellona Arsenal. While it superficially appeared that the author of the article anticipated the later naming of the site in honor of the sister of the god of war, it is highly probable that the government's purchase was a part of this tract. Thus, a century before its use as an arsenal, this section was settled permanently.[95] By August 1816, work on the main buildings was well advanced, and reparations were made to begin the construction of the powder magazine. It had been decided to locate the magazine on the eastern side of the hill, where the arsenal itself was to stand.

Since this was the side that faced Bellona Foundry, which was 250 yards away, the major immediately became alarmed for the safety of his property. The plan was to make the arsenal a quadrangle, with machine shops housed in brick buildings on both the east and the west sides, a soldiers' barracks on the north side, bachelor officers' quarters in the northeast and northwest corners and a commanding officer's residence on the south. A stone wall filled in the spaces between the buildings, and less than 100 yards away was the powder magazine, the massive dual-stone walls of which are still standing.[96]

Fearing that an explosion in such close quarters would blast his expensive installations into ruble and perhaps kill a large number of his labor force, Clarke protested immediately to Washington. He pointed out several detailed technical objections, but he was also careful to remind Colonel Bomford of his efforts in procuring the site. The powder magazine was accordingly moved to the western side of the hill, some fifty yards beyond the arsenal's quadrangle. Every effort was made to render this structure as blast-proof as

Charcoal drawing of Bellona. *Courtesy of the University of Virginia Archives.*

Bellona Arsenal's remaining three-story building in the 1900s. It is now half of a home. *Courtesy of the Library of Congress.*

possible; it was built of tightly cemented masonry, and its windowless walls were as much as five and half feet thick. The whole arsenal was surrounded by a stone wall that rose well above the magazine's roof. With such safeguards, all of Clarke's objections must have been answered and all his fears allayed. There were two explosions in the vicinity in later years, but they were not at the powder magazine.

Erected at a cost of $250,000, the arsenal mainly served as a repository for the cannons that were being turned out next door at Clarke's foundry, but they also served as a place to fabricate and repair small arms. It was built in 1816 by the government as an army post, and the nearby foundry supplied the military in the antebellum era. During the Civil War, the complex served the Confederacy. The Luck family renovated the three remaining buildings in the early 1940s.[97] The construction of the arsenal continued throughout the rest of 1816 and into 1817. The completed installation consisted of a walled enclosure with eight brick buildings inside. The two largest buildings were the main arsenal, which was three stories tall and situated on the north side of the quadrangle, and the equally high barracks on the south. Two of the remaining six structures, which were designed as officers' quarters, flanked to the main arsenal. Four others, which were used as workshops and storerooms, were located between the arsenal and the barracks; two of these were on the eastern side and the other two were on the western side of the compound.

Security was provided by not only the seventeen-foot-tall brick wall that connected the buildings but also by iron gratings on all outside windows, the double-planked wooden gates and the loopholes (small holes in the brick to fire a rifle) in the walls of every structure. The gun ports in the main arsenal were large enough to permit the use of cannons. The bricks used in the arsenal and magazine were made on the site, and the stone, according to local stories, was capstone from the coal mines (capstone was the stone that covered the coal). Frank Woodson, in 1912, said that the roof was made of stone brought from Maine and covered with slate.[98]

Substantial buildings of brick and stone were erected by the government. On two of the site's stones were the words: "Commenced January 1816. Finished October 1817. James Madison, president, Ames Munford, colonel of ordnance, George Bomford, lieutenant of ordnance, military department; Robert Lecky, master mason; James Walford, master builder; Andrew Fagan and Josiah P. Pierce, master carpenters." The buildings on the east side were used for the storage of cannons and small arms; those on the west side were used as the hospital and workshops. The barracks were placed immediately at the front of a quadrangle and covered 3.5 acres,

Left: A 1950 image of the Bellona Arsenal property. *Courtesy of the* Times-Dispatch *newspaper.*

Below: One stone-engraved plaque over the fireplace at Bellona. *Courtesy of the Library of Virginia.*

and at the rear of this line was the largest building, where the officers' quarters and post headquarters were housed.

Except for the latter, which was a frame-built structure, the buildings were built from brick, with walls that were three feet thick at certain heights and supported by massive foundations of stone. Rock from Maine was brought in to build the powder magazine beneath the hill. The inner walls were thick enough for three men to walk abreast. All the roofs were made of slate capped with lead, and the buildings were connected by a brick wall that was pierced at regular intervals with portholes where cannons were counted and extended to the top stories.

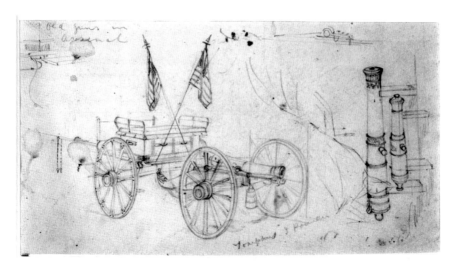

A drawing of a cannon carrying cart with flags, 1810–14. *Courtesy of the Library of Congress.*

While the arsenal was being built, the War of 1812 tension had passed. The militiamen were all back on their farms, and May's Tavern in Manchester was the place where they presented their claims for pay.[99] From 1816 to 1821, the post was garrisoned by a small detachment of ordnance troops. Then, a company of artillery was assigned to duty there. From that time until Bellona was discontinued as an active post, this arm of the service bore the responsibility of its maintenance. The arsenal was garrisoned by a company of U.S. Artillery. Besides being a depot for a number of military stores, the arsenal had a number of artificers who were employed to repair and fabricate small arms and other munitions of war. The U.S. officers at the Bellona Arsenal constructed many big guns before they were boated downriver to the deck of a sailing ship at Rockets Landing, where it was transported to Fort Monroe at Old Point Comfort.[100]

Under acts of Congress from March 3, 1819, and April 18, 1828, steps were taken by the government to abolish Bellona Arsenal, but it was not until March 3, 1853, that Jefferson Davis, the secretary of war, sold the land to Phillip St. George Cocke. The small garrison was maintained until the early 1940s. The orders that were received to transfer arsenal activities to Fort Monroe were numerous; the continuous expense and inconvenience of transportation and the extreme difficulty in obtaining and retaining the mechanics were just a few of the arsenal's issues. The order also addressed the unsafe situation of the property in that it was close to the coal pits

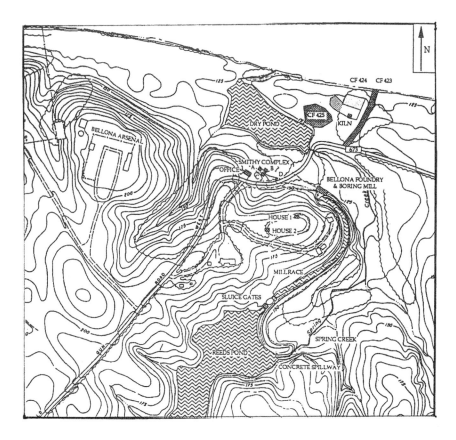

The Bellona complex. An engineer's 1865 map of the entire Bellona area. *Courtesy of the Chesterfield County Library, drawn in 1992.*

and a great number of rebellious "negroes." The arsenal was located in the middle of an area in which slaves were relatively numerous, and the civilians were exceptionally nervous. They had recurring fears of a servile insurrection and were periodically plagued by those responsible for the arsenal's protection. Neighbors feared that the nearby Midlothian coal fields, where several thousand stalwart bondsmen were employed, were a potential source of trouble.

One of the reasons for the arsenal's location was its close proximity of over five thousand slaves; it was there to prevent potential revolts, which were realized in the nearly successful Gabriel's Rebellion and Nat Turner's Rebellion, which happened in Southampton County, Virginia, in August 1831.[101] Gabriel Prosser's slave conspiracy, planned for 1800, ended in

In 1810 Major John Clarke and noted Richmond lawyer, William Wirt, established a weapons factory for the U.S. War Department on the south bank of the James River five miles north of here. Bellona Arsenal, (named for the Roman goddess of war,) was erected in 1816. After five years of disuse, it was leased to Thomas Mann Randolph in 1837 (for use as a silk worm farm.) Junius L. Archer bought the property in 1856, and on January 1, 1863, he leased both the arsenal and foundry to the Confederate government. Bellona Arsenal became one of Virginia's leading producers of arms.

Top: A Bellona cannon and cannon mold recovered from the James River and three remaining arsenal buildings. *Courtesy of the Chesterfield County Library.*

Bottom: Bellona Arsenal Highway Marker 0-40 at the intersection of Route 60 and Robious Road, 1810–63. *Photograph courtesy of M. Robinson.*

severe repression. While no whites were killed in the revolt that never really got started, the State of Virginia executed, by public hanging, twenty-seven blacks, including Gabriel. Nat Turner's rebellion, in 1831, was one of the bloodiest and most effective slave revolts in American history. The Virginia General Assembly had an improbable debate about the abolition of slavery in Virginia. Turner ignited a culture of fear in Virginia that eventually spread to the rest of the South. Governor Thomas Mann Randolph[102] shared these anxieties, and in 1821, Randolph protested to the secretary of war about the lax defenses at Bellona. His successor, James Pleasants Jr., made a similar complaint two years later. Although these fears never materialized, they did produce an unhealthy atmosphere of suspicion and tension.

As if this were not enough, a high rate of sickness in the garrison prevailed from the beginning. Some type of fever, possibly malaria, was responsible, but Bellona's lack of a proper infirmary also seems to have contributed to the post's bad record. No effective steps were taken to remedy these conditions, as the medical authorities of the day were inclined to blame the harmful "miamas" that were supposed to rise from the water and to infect the air. The commander was therefore ordered to plant a grove of trees between the arsenal and the river "in order that the miamas may be more certainly carried over the buildings."[103]

What's Hidden on the Seven Hills in Richmond?

1750–1865

The "Seven Hills" in the City of Richmond (chartered in 1742) during this period were:

Gamble's Hill
Union Hill
Council Chamber Hill
French Garden Hill
Navy Hill
Shockoe Hill
Church Hill[104]

Gamble's Hill 1798–1865

Gamble's Hill Residential in Richmond

The Gamble's Hill location, in the period between the 1750s and the American Civil War, included significant sections within one of the Seven Hills in Richmond, Virginia. The historically developed locations within Gamble's Hill were named Oregon Hill (original subdivision, now the War Memorial), James River, Kanawha Canal and Basin, Tredegar Iron Works, Gamble's Hill (residential), Latrobe's Prison, the Virginia Manufactory of Arms (Richmond Arsenal) and Neilsons Island (now called Brown's Island).

Richmond map from 1864 that lists each of the seven recognized hills of Richmond. *Map courtesy of the City of Richmond, U.S. Coast Guard, 1864.* These are the names of the Seven Hills by number.

1. Union Hill 2. Council Chamber Hill 3. French Garden Hill 4. Navy Hill 5. Gambles Hill 6. Shockoe Hill 7. Church Hill

Of the Seven Hills in the city of Richmond, around the middle of the 1700s, one of the most important and remembered was Gamble's Hill. Only a portion of one building exists today, but the hidden stories about the buildings and people that made it significant have been lost.

Today, Ethyl Corporation now occupies six acres of property atop Gamble's Hill, along with their neighbors the Virginia War Memorial. And, at the bottom of the hill is the remains of the Tredegar Iron Works building,

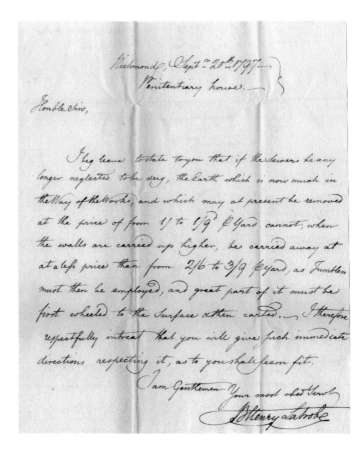

Original penitentiary building instructions by Latrobe from 1797. *Courtesy of the Library of Virginia.*

which has be transformed into headquarters for the American Civil War Museum and Historic Tredegar. The Kanawha Canal still runs along the Tredegar building, and Brown's Island on the James River is now used for concerts and entertainment.

PRATT'S CASTLE OR GREY'S CASTLE

1800–1880

In 1800, the magnificent home Greys Castle was built for Colonel John Harvie, a Revolutionary patriot and Virginia aristocrat. Harvie was a Revolutionary War veteran, the city's fourth mayor and a signer of the Articles of Confederation. The Castle was designed by Benjamin Latrobe, the architect of the Richmond Penitentiary and, later, the Capitol in

Washington; his drawings of the mansion are now in the Library of Congress. The colonel was a member of the Continental Convention of 1775.

On Whitsunday, May 24, 1607, a week after landing at Jamestown, Captain Newport, Captain John Smith, Gabriel Archer and the Honorable George Percy went to Richmond to explore the new country.[105] A town was started at the falls of the James River 130 years later, and over 60 more years passed before Colonel Robert Gamble took up his residence on this fine site and thus gave it its name.

Born in Augusta County in 1754, Colonel Gamble served in the Revolution and moved to Richmond in 1792. There, he became one of its most prominent merchants. Gamble married Catherine, the daughter of Major John Gratton, who had made herself as famous for her courage as she was for her beauty by riding through the country at night warning the settlers on the border of her neighborhood of an impending Native American raid. Gamble died in 1810, and his widow continued to occupy the mansion until her death in 1832.

The Gamble girls attracted many suitors, but Elizabeth loved only William Wirt, "who was talented and had good looks, was a lawyer, author, attorney general and chancellor of Virginia, and soon the hand of Elizabeth." Elizabeth's sister Agnes was just as beautiful and later married William H. Cabell, the governor of Virginia, in 1805. William's place was sold to Colonel Gamble, who named his acquisition Grey's Castle. Immediately to the right of Gamble's Hill was Cunningham's Pond, which was formally a basin of the James River Canal that supplied Cunningham's Mill, later Tredegar Iron Works. And of course, in front of the house, between the canal and the river, stood the old Virginia Armory, which was built in 1805. To the west, between Harvie's Mill Pond and Gallows' Hill, Fourth Street was then merely a series of gullies. After the Wirts moved away, Judge and Mrs. Cabell became the sole master and mistress of the house and dispensers of its hospitality.

Before Colonel Gamble's death, similar cottages were already being replaced by substantial brick houses. One of the later houses, which was just across Third Street from the Chevallie House, was built about 1812 and was the home of Benjamin Watkins Leigh, the distinguished jurist. In the years before he married his third wife, the daughter of John Wickham, Leigh moved into the house his farther-in-law had built at the corner of Tenth and Clay Streets.[106]

By 1852, the stuccoed Gamble Manor passed from its heirs and was called the White House or Gray Castle. Of course, William Wirt was the direct

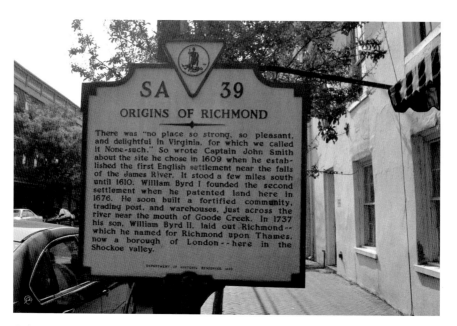

Origins of Richmond SA 39. The second settlement of John Smith was established here in 1676. *Photograph courtesy of M. Robinson.*

The Virginia Manufactory of Arms before a fire during the Civil War in 1865. *Courtesy of* The Armory Scandal, *Davie C. Poteet, Library of Virginia.*

partner of Major John Clarke in the building and construction of Bellona in Midlothian, Virginia. Before the Civil War, Gamble's Hill was probably the only park in central Richmond and was the home of Charles Wallace. Later, a book collector named John McGuire Sr. had his famous university there, but it was torn down in 1888.[107]

LATROBE'S PRISON ON THE JAMES

The First Penitentiary at Gamble's Hill

The first penitentiary was also designed by Benjamin Latrobe, and its construction was aided by Major John Clarke. The Virginia General Assembly, in 1796, authorized construction of the penitentiary. Governor Wood selected Benjamin Latrobe as the architect and Thomas Giles as the superintendent. It was built on twelve acres on the James River in the Gamble's Hill area of Richmond. The Virginia Penitentiary was opened in 1800. Latrobe's design, while architecturally impressive, was functionally flawed. The cells were large enough to hold several prisoners; however, the cell doors had no windows, making it impossible to supervise the prisoners. In addition, the cells had no heat, poor ventilation and no plumbing. Prisoners also had to eat in these conditions since the penitentiary did not have a dining room.

The penitentiary's day-to-day operations were overseen by a keeper (or superintendent), who was appointed by the governor for a one-year term,

Original picture of the first penitentiary building, circa 1797. *Courtesy of* The Powell Project, *2015.*

Left: Virginia State Penitentiary sign SA 113, located on Belvedere Street. *Photograph courtesy of M. Robinson.*

Right: Latrobe Penitentiary on the James River in 1800. *Courtesy of the Library of Virginia.*

and deputies were appointed by the keeper. A board of twelve inspectors, who were appointed by the Hustings Court of the City of Richmond, oversaw penitentiary operations. In 1819, the general assembly abolished the board of inspectors and created a five-person board of directors (later reduced to three members who were appointed by the governor; the keeper was still appointed by the governor). An 1852 act gave the general assembly the power to elect a superintendent for a two-year term.

Early on the morning of April 3, 1865, the final day of the federal occupation, the convicts were awakened by the sounds of explosions from the destruction of the powder magazine and the James River Squadron. When they realized that the guards were no longer at their posts, the convicts broke out of their cells and set themselves free. They stole civilian clothes from the prison store house, plundered some buildings, set the prison workshop on fire and then left to join the mobs in search of food and booty. However, for most, freedom was short-lived. With the Union came the provost marshal and infantry, which restored order as quickly as possible. Later that morning, a dragnet was thrown over the city, and all suspicious characters were rounded up. By nightfall, most of the convicts were back behind bars. More than one hundred were held in Libby Prison or Castle Thunder until the penitentiary could be repaired.[108]

Latrobe's original structure was torn down in 1928.

VIRGINIA STATE PENITENTIARY

1797

Latrobe's first major project in the United States was the State Penitentiary in Richmond, which was commissioned in 1797. The penitentiary (1796–1991) implemented many innovative ideas in penal reform that were espoused by Thomas Jefferson and other figures, including cells arranged in a semicircle, which was similar but not identical to Jeremy Bentham's panopticon (a prison arranged so that all parts of the interior are visible from a single point) and allowed for easy surveillance. It also improved living conditions for sanitation and ventilation. He also pioneered the use of solitary confinement in the Richmond Penitentiary.

When it received its first prisoners in 1800, the Virginia State Penitentiary had, through a series of radical redesigns, grown from architect Benjamin Latrobe's elegant horseshoe-shaped loggia on the banks of the James River into an enormous modern complex of cellblocks and administrative buildings. The structure was mostly constructed with inmate labor, and it was partly built with the brick and stone of Latrobe's original horseshoe, which had itself fallen into disuse and was razed in 1928.

The Virginia State Penitentiary[109] (1796–1991), which has been demolished, was Latrobe's first major public commission in America, and it was a monument to the era's penal reform movement. Latrobe's elevations of the south front of the proposed prison building showed an entryway and a

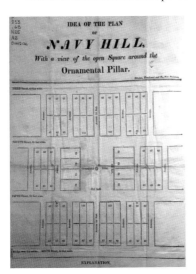

An idea for the plan of Navy Hill Square that was never completed in 1816. *Courtesy of the Library of Virginia.*

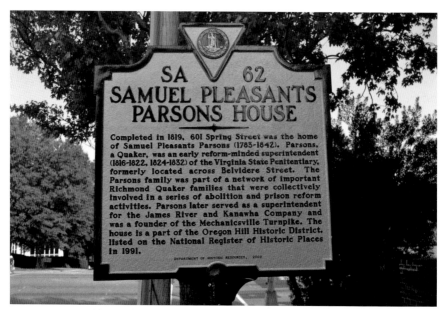

Above: Samuel Parsons House in 1819. The supervisor of penitentiary and a Quaker family built the home on Spring Street. *Photograph courtesy of M. Robinson.*

Left: Pratt's Castle on Gambles Hill was a Richmond Landmark built in 1853; it is now demolished. *Courtesy of the Library of Congress.*

"keeper's house" at the center of the ranges of cells. The plan reflects the Enlightenment era's reliance on solitary confinement and surveillance as a way to reform prisoners. Throughout most of the eighteenth century, the reform of criminals was thought impossible, so public ostracism and severe punishments were routine. The reformers hoped that criminals could redeem themselves through penitence and solitary reflection.

Latrobe's plan also called for the separation of male and female prisoners—a practice seldom followed in earlier jails. In completing the prison's solemn and imposing main entrance, Latrobe adapted elements from English architect George Dance's design for Newgate Prison, especially the stark festoons of chains bracketing the inscription over the passageway. The design detail was, however, not included in the construction of the building, which was completed by Major John Clarke after Latrobe left Virginia in 1798. Only seven sheets of Latrobe's design for the Virginia prison survived.[110]

In 1794, Major John Clarke built the state armory at Gamble's Hill and Latrobe's State Penitentiary. Clarke was also appointed the superintendent of the state armory in 1798 and was also connected with the Virginia State Arsenal in Richmond.

KANAWHA CANAL AT GAMBLE'S HILL

The Richmond and Gamble's Hill sections of the city had a very unique experience with a canal running through the areas. And it is also unusual to have a canal, a pond and a turning basin in the Gamble's Hill area. Some people called this water the Penitentiary Pond, which was in the area bounded by Second Street, Gamble's Hill and Tredegar Iron Works. The pond was built some time before 1800; however, it was filled in around late 1880s.

As one looks at the map of 1877, one can see Harvey's Pond, which was George Washington's vision of a waterway to the west. It was a small turning basin with a wharf located in the wedge-shaped valley between Oregon Hill and Gamble's Hill. Again, the canal was the brainchild of George Washington, and through his influence, the canal was chartered in 1785. The initial survey of the canal established the idea of the Richmond water level extending from the foot of Ninth Street to a point three miles upriver, where the river could be navigated by bateau.

The eastern limit of the Lower Level, the Great Turning Basin between Seventh and Twelfth Streets, opened in 1800. Construction of the canal also created Harvie's Pond east of the present location of the Brown's Island Way. When the pond was named, it had a variety of referenced names; the several names were the Pond (*Young Map of Richmond*, 1800), Harvie's Pond (*Bates Map of the City of Richmond*, 1835), the Basin (*Ellyson Map of the City of Richmond*, 1858), Penitentiary Pond (*Pleasants Map of the Lower Level of the Lower Section of the James River and Kanawha Canal*, 1868) and the Basin (*Illustrated Atlas of the City of Richmond*, 1877). The basin was carved from land originally owned by Lewis E. Harvie, whose property was adjacent to the basin.[111]

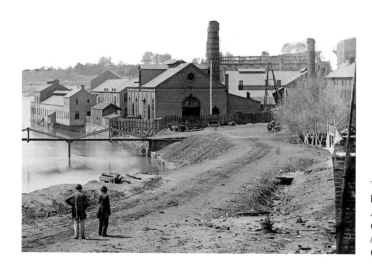

The Tredegar buildings in April 1865. *Courtesy of the Library of Congress.*

In 1847, the Harvie family platted the original Oregon Hill subdivision east of what is now Belvidere Street and South of Spring Street. Over time, the entire area of Belvidere Hill came to be referred to as Oregon Hill. In the following years, Harvie's Pond was modified, and the canal received improvements. An 1823–25 reconstruction changed the existing width of the canal and towpath. The 1838 reconstruction introduced changes in depth and width and added an eight-foot granite retaining wall.

Harvie's Mill Pond Basin, or Penitentiary Pond, began as a turnaround for canal boats immediately prior to 1800. "The Upper Basin seems to have been in use even before the Great Basin was finished downtown."[112] The Upper Basin designation lends a utilitarian dignity to the quaint, personal description of Harvie's Mill Pond, which was named for Colonel John Harvie, who died in 1810. Harvie owned considerable acreage in that section of town. Harvie Street in the Fan is named for his family. The Upper Basin was a center of activity. Around it was a tanning yard, a coal yard and a gauge dock for determining canal-boat tolls. "Tolls were the only way the canal company made money but getting the exact weight doesn't appear to have been their great concern; problem was, the canal only had a 3-foot depth. The boat wouldn't get through if it weighed too much."[113] Today it is a parcel of green, rolling ground between the Virginia War Memorial and the Ethyl Corporation campus.[114]

JOSEPH REID ANDERSON

1841–Civil War

In 1841, the owners turned management of Tredegar Iron Works over to a twenty-eight-year-old civil engineer named Joseph Reed Anderson, who proved to be an able manager. Anderson acquired ownership of the foundry in 1848, after two years of leasing the works, and he was soon doing work for the United States government. Anderson began introducing slave labor to cut production costs. By the beginning of the Civil War in 1861, half of Tredegar's nine hundred workers were slaves, including many who were in skilled positions. By 1860, Anderson's father-in-law, Dr. Robert Archer, had joined the business, and Tredegar became a leading iron producer in the country.

On May 15, 1863, a fire also swept through the Tredegar complex, severely damaging several buildings, including the boring mill, which necessitated the removal of a number of cannons to the nearby Richmond Naval Ordnance Works near Rocket's Landing for the purposes of boring and finishing. The same fire also destroyed Tredegar's locomotive shop, a blacksmith shop and several other adjacent machine shops and small foundry-support buildings.

The Union capture of nearby Petersburg on April 2, 1865, triggered the evacuation of Richmond, and the next day, a fire raged through the city, destroying one-third of it, including the arsenal. Much of the Tredegar Iron Works was spared because the owner employed a large number of guards to ward off any arsonists.

A drawing of the front of the penitentiary building in the 1800s. *Courtesy of J.R. Hamilton, artist.*

James River Area at Gamble's Hill

It was difficult to cross the James River at the Gamble's Hill area because of the two islands (Nelsons Island, the Belle Island and the spillway in between). Around 1865, there were only a few ways to cross the James River from Gamble's Hill area or any other area from Richmond. By April 1865, there was a pontoon two-lane bridge over the James River, near Gamble's Hill. This was a two-lane wooded bridge positioned over many pontoons that allowed pedestrians and certain vehicles to cross the James River. There were small sections of these bridges that could be removed and moved out of the way to allow boats to maneuver through the pontoon sections of the bridge.

The only permanent bridge that allowed vehicles to cross the river during this time was the Old Mayo Bridge (built in 1788), which was named after John Mayo; it was also later rebuilt and is now called the Mayo or Fourteenth Street Bridge. The remaining two bridges that existed during this time (1865) were the two railroad bridges. The Mayo Bridge was used to evacuate citizens who were escaping the burning of the city by the North at the end of the Civil War. The railroad bridges were operated for the Richmond & Petersburg Railroad and the Richmond & Danville Railroad.

Brown's Island Dam, which was located at the upstream end of the island, spans the entire river and directs water into the head gates across Haxall Canal. Power from Brown's Island began running electric streetcars in 1894, when Richmond Railway & Electric built a coal-fired generating plant. In 1888, Richmond became the first city in the world to successfully run an electric streetcar system.

Union Hill

Union Hill was so named because it was a hill that was united or joined with Church Hill by roads and bridges in the 1800s. Street grading in the nineteenth century joined the two hills, giving the neighborhood its name. Today, residents say they welcome new development but that it should reflect the architectural history of the area. Home to antebellum, Victorian, Classical Revival and modern architecture, Union Hill is in the Virginia Landmarks Register and the National Register of Historic Places. The neighborhood has awesome historic housing stock but nothing

Union Hill, overlooking the city of Richmond. *Photograph courtesy of M. Robinson.*

grandiose. The community is evolving, for the most part, in the way it was intended: as workforce housing with a diverse socioeconomic base. Most of the neighbors want to see the development of empty lots, but it should be appropriate to a historic district.

Union Hill was roughly defined as being between North Twenty-Fifth Streets and Jefferson Avenue, which are located in the east end of the City of Richmond. For much of its history, Union Hill was separated from the city and the rest of Church Hill by a deep ravine and bluffs overlooking Shockoe Valley. The streets on Union Hill follow the terrain rather than the rigid grid of the rest of the city; the angled streets of Union Hill collide with the city's grid in interesting triangular blocks. This gives Union Hill a unique character found nowhere else in the city.

Union Hill has a unique neighborhood; it sits between Church Hill and a ravine, where Interstate 95 currently runs. Union Hill was separated from most of the other neighborhoods because of its roads, which created a uniquely diverse and independent community. Most of the community's homes are as uniquely shaped as the streets; they are often seen in various trapezoidal and rectangular shapes, which are irregular in comparison to the other neighborhoods in Richmond. However, most of these homes were demolished in 1940s. The only home from this period that is still standing today is the Adam Miller House. Built in 1824, it is a two-story Flemish-bond brick dwelling on a raised foundation that was owned by local farmer Adam Miller. Although the house burned in the 1870s, it was repaired and still stands in its full glory at 2410 Venable Street.

Union Hill is primarily a residential district, with a few churches and commercial buildings, concentrated along Twenty-Fifth and Venable Streets. The dwellings, which are constructed of frame and brick, are modest, working-class houses, and many of them were built prior to 1867, when Union Hill was annexed from Henrico County. Today, Union Hill is a fragile neighborhood suffering from abandonment and neglect.

Topography did more to shape the character of Union Hill than anything else. The cliffs overlooking Shockoe Valley formed the western edge of the neighborhood, while a deep ravine that cut diagonally from the corner of Broad and Twentieth Streets to North and Twenty-Fourth Streets defined the southern limits; the land in between was hilly and rugged. In 1805, when John Adams and Benjamin Mosby laid out Union Hill for development, they used an irregular street pattern to accommodate the hilly terrain. "They used a grid pattern, but instead of a rigid plan with equal size squares, like that of Richmond, the grid was adapted to curve and climb with the hills. This resulted in several narrow, bending streets, and squares of various sizes and shapes. The terrain also isolated the community from the rest of Church Hill and the city."

Well into the 1830s, "Union Hill was almost a wilderness with a sparse population." A single family controlled much of Union Hill for the first quarter of the nineteenth century, limiting development to the base of Venable Street, where it begins its ascent from Shockoe Valley, and on the bluffs above. The earliest-known house on Union Hill was that of Henry Mettert. Mettert built his house at the corner of Venable and Eighteenth Streets sometime between 1805 and 1810. Following the angle of the intersection, the two-story brick dwelling formed an obtuse angle. However, this home was demolished in 1940.

In 1820, Richmond had a population of 12,067. By 1860, the city's population had grown to 37,910, and Richmond had become the third most affluent city in the nation. The city's prosperity and growth were led by three industries: tobacco, flour and iron. By 1835, the city's industrial growth resulted in a demand for housing, both by the factory owners and workers. During this period, it became profitable for the heirs of Richard Adams II to subdivide and sell their holdings on Union Hill. Most of the new houses were the modest dwellings of working-class people, including tailors, tanners, butchers, coach makers, teamsters, mechanics, painters and carpenters. Union Hill's more affluent residents, such as Elijah Baker, Frederick Brauer, George W. Barker, Joseph Augustine, Robert Alvis, Daniel von Groning and Jesse Talbott, built many houses as investments. Nearly eighty buildings from this period still stand on Union Hill. Unfortunately, an equal number have disappeared in the past few decades. The only nonresidential building from this period that still exists is Union Hill Chapel (later Asbury Chapel), which was built in 1843 at 812 North Twenty-Fifth Street to serve the community's growing Methodist congregation.

The massive development that occurred on Union Hill during the 1840s and 1850s began to wane in the 1860s. As with the rest of the city and the South, building materials were scarce, and focus turned to winning the war.

ANTEBELLUM PERIOD

1830–1860

The antebellum period witnessed tremendous expansion in the City of Richmond and on Union Hill. Slaves moved into free black neighborhoods as the practice of boarding out increased in the 1850s. This shift was the result of Richmond's increased industrialization. Union Hill was one such area, where blacks lived among whites in an integrated neighborhood.

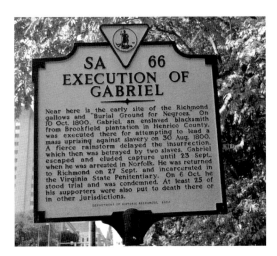

The execution of Gabriel in 1800. Gabriel, a black slave who led an uprising against slavery, was caught and hung. *Photograph courtesy of M. Robinson.*

Such networks of urban slaves competed and cooperated with the free black population in cities like Richmond, and their interactions created a substantial economy that was unintended by the architects of the system. By the mid-1830s, one thousand hired enslaved African Americans were living out and enjoying a type of quasi-freedom in Richmond. And at night, they settled in among the nearly two thousand free African Americans in a city of eighteen thousand. By the mid-1840s, several thousand enslaved laborers had scattered themselves among the free black population, who supplied them with food and lodging in every part of the city.[115]

COUNCIL CHAMBER HILL

Council Chamber Hill was an unusually dense neighborhood that occupied a small spur that protrudes from Shockoe Hill and the steeply falling ground around it just east of Capitol Square. It commanded a dramatic view of the Shockoe Valley and of the James River. The hill was usually included in lists of the Seven Hills of Richmond, and it was a dark figure in the accounts of some of the city's most colorful history. Today, it is mostly a parking lot that is banked above the broad barrenness of the relocated Fourteenth Street and surrounded by aging office towers. Most assume that it is hard to find anything in the deserted asphalt behind the labyrinthine bulk of the State Highway Department Headquarters, but most underestimate the resistance of the urban fabric falling into utter oblivion.

This neighborhood, which was still extant when Mary Wingfield Scott wrote in the 1940s, was largely obliterated in the expansion of state office facilities during the mid-century. Council Chamber Hill is hardly remembered today, but it was once best known for its demi-monde character as Richmond's red-light district during the Civil War. Looking west along Ross Street, one can see the dip or ravine between Council Chamber and Shockoe Hill, up which Governor Street runs. The region east of the governor's mansion was a haven for bawdy houses, gambling dens and houses of prostitution during the years before 1865, when a reformer disrupted their activities. Arabella Yarrington Worsham met her future husband, railroad tycoon Colis P. Huntington, at Johnny Worsham's gambling establishment on Fourteenth Street on Council Chamber Hill. According to Mary Wingfield Scott, Worsham later operated a faro bank in an antebellum house that stood on the lot to the right.

Governor's Mansion plaque, 1813. The mansion was designed by architect Alexander Parris. *Photograph courtesy of M. Robinson.*

The Governor's Mansion, built in 1813, was the oldest purpose-built residence for governors. *Photograph courtesy of M. Robinson.*

Ross Street is a tributary of today's Governor Street, the "county road" in the eighteenth and early nineteenth centuries that connected the original town east of Shockoe Creek with the new platted area on the hill. The county road is the curving route that dashes to the north of the "public square" and east of Twelfth Street. The land atop Council Chamber Hill was apparently acquired from the Byrd family before the newer section of town was platted. It is seen as the blank section in the center of the upper area of the detail from an 1809 map attributed to Richard Young; Governor Street (now called County Road) can be seen to the west, and Shockoe Creek, which ran west of Seventeenth Street on the plat, can be seen to the east. Thus, it was not laid out in streets at first, although its steep geography would have stymied development for a long time had it been laid out as a continuation of the overall grid.

Colonel John Mayo, the builder of the eponymous bridge over the James River, lived in a brick house that was built as the interim seat of the governor's council and executive offices; it also gave its name to the hill. Mayo is said to have kept a close eye on the condition of his ramshackle bridge by the use of a spyglass from his house on the hill.

The proximity of this hill to the capitol had made it, from an early date, a logical location for boardinghouses. In 1841, such small enterprises were eclipsed by the building of the Exchange Hotel at Fourteenth and Franklin Streets. When it was opened on July 1, 1841, no detail of its appearance was spared. The Exchange Hotel had a stimulating effect on the area, particularly on lower Franklin Street. As the nineteenth century progressed and property values increased, John Mayo felt called to develop much of the area. He did this by creating a series of narrow lots on tiers of streets and alleys that stepped down the hill to the east and the south. These can be seen on the detail from the map by Richard Young from 1817. The undeveloped portion of the hill containing the Mayo House is marked J. Mayo. The original bed of Shockoe Creek is the curving stream to the right, Ross Street is to the left and Monumental Church can be seen in the upper left corner. Fourteenth Street was later extended up the hill to Broad Street.

Jessica Bankston has explored the likelihood that the watercolor illustration for one of Latrobe's most elegant villas was intended for the Mayo family on Council Chamber Hill, as she has documented on her blog. In a useful map, she was able to determine the modern location of Clifton by applying a section of the *1876 F.W. Beers Map* to an aerial photo of the area. Her map indicates how dense Council Chamber Hill had become by the late nineteenth century.

For many decades after 1843, this Clifton building, together with a large annex, was used as a boardinghouse called the Clifton House. In 1889, the owner, Dr. Booth of Carter's Grove, lent the house, which was then in very deteriorated condition, to the Sheltering Arms Hospital, which occupied the building until it moved to the Grant house on Clay four years later. The Clifton House was demolished in 1905.[116] The only remaining (relatively modern) building from the neighborhood and the foundation of a successor building that stood on the site of Clifton, an easily recognized building that Bankston believes was based on the plans for the unbuilt Mayo villa, can be found here.

On the fatal day of April 3, 1865, when the doomed Confederate government ordered the tobacco warehouses to be fired on in order to keep their contents out of the enemy's hands, the neighborhood between Ninth and Fifteenth Street was lost forever.

The Exchange Hotel, Richmond's most architecturally sophisticated hotel from the antebellum era, once stood on the north edge of what is now the modern extension of Bank Street. Today, not one brick remains of the Old Council Chamber Hill.

FRENCH GARDEN HILL

French Garden Hill was so named because a Frenchman named Didier Colin had a beautiful garden and a small amusement park on this hill. In 1792, Colin bought nearly nineteen acres of land and opened an amusement park called the French Garden. Colin was a wigmaker who loved and plied his trade on Main Street, just west of Shockoe Creek.[117] Today, one can best visualize the remote settlement of the 1840s and 1850s by walking to the northern ends of Eighth, Ninth and Tenth Streets, which still run two blocks north of Leigh Street before ending in a steep and rugged ravine. There is not much hope today that the desolate hillside overlooking the CSX tracks will ever be more than an ironic caricature of the wigmaker's French Garden.[118]

Many inquiries have been made over the years about the history of the old house that stood on the hillside above the tracks of Seaboard Railway on Abigail Street, at the upper end of Ninth Street. It was a strongly built structure with a granite first story and two stories above the thick foundation. From the passengers who rode the trains of the Chesapeake and Ohio

Railway, which ran to and from Richmond, there were many speculations about the home, as it had the appearance of a deserted castle in some medieval setting in ancient France. Very recently, this old villa was razed, and Richmond lost another on the long list of destroyed historic shrines. Only the granite first story remains at this time—the last of the homes of the French refugees from the shambles of Santo Domingo.

These refugees fled as a result of the insurrection of the slaves in that French colony. These refugees scattered in many directions, and the ones who went to Richmond were hospitably received by its citizens. They settled along the Shockoe Valley, which became known as French Garden Hill. This settlement was founded in the year 1793, and in due course, the hills around the north end of Richmond were inevitably covered with the grape vines of the Frenchmen. As an artistic people, the French soon made their grounds beautiful with flowers and shrubs. The records shows the names of some of these refugees, including DuQuesne, Colin, Delarue, Chevallie and many others, and Richmond has never had reason to regret the initial reception of them.

As the Native Americans retreated toward the Blue Ridge, settlers appeared around the Shockoe Valley, and it then became the land of Nathaniel Bacon, who was later known as a glorious rebel, but upon his untimely death, the lands were forfeited or escheated. On October 25, 1773, Sir William Berkeley, as the governor and captain-general of the colony and in the name of His Majesty King Charles the Second, it became the property of William Byrd, the elder; the grant made up about ten thousand acres. It was then purchased by Colonel John Mayo, whose daughter Maria became the bride of General Scott.

The old home of French refugee Didier Colin stood there from the 1790s until 1939. This "remote suburb" is now only about seven squares from the state capitol. Didier Colin purchased this land from Dr. Philip Turpin,[119] and the locality became known as the French Garden. The ownership of the property then passed to the Seaboard Railway. Only one other former owner could be found: Miss Sue Douthat. The property was left to her by Dr. William Price Palmer, one of the most popular Richmond physicians before the war. Because the law in 1829 required voters to own real property, John V. Hardwick, in 1847, sold the property to twenty-eight residents of the city so that they might have suffrage rights. The land was laid out in twenty-eight lots; in 1859, a portion of the land was sold to Dr. Palmer.

Linden Waller gave a lively description of French Garden Hill before its development as a residence section:

There was one small brick house occupied by a (colored) woman who used to have a tame coon chained to a tree. All around the brow of the hill was to be seen the remains of old fortifications. From the eastern side of the hill, from the top to the bottom, were large pine trees, and we boys used to have our pranks and slide over the pine tags to the bottom.
—Mary Wingfield Scott, Valentine Museum[120]

The old villa became known as No. 916 Abigail Street. It was used as a Confederate hospital, as it was quite adaptable for such a purpose, with three stories and twelve to fifteen rooms. The location of this villa in French Garden Hill was a charming site before the war, when the limpid stream was known as Bacon's Quarter Branch. This hillside was a glowing fairyland, and the area just north of the home was called the White House of the Confederacy.

If the French Garden Hills were embellished like Gamble's Hill, travelers entering the city on the railroads would be impressed by the initial views of these hills, and they would anticipate all the city has to offer in beauty, romance and history.

NAVY HILL

The Navy Hill neighborhood, which was named as a tribute to nearby naval victories during the War of 1812, was settled by German immigrants beginning in 1810. It became a vibrant African American community by the turn of the century. Navy Hill's distinctive character was embodied by the buildings there, between North Third and Thirteenth Streets. Today, Navy Hill is a downtown area that is ripe for tremendous development, and the Richmond mayor has just unveiled a failed $1.5 billion proposal to redevelop the area around the Richmond Coliseum. The plan calls for a 17,500-seat arena; a high-rise hotel; 2,500 apartments; 1 million square feet for office, commercial and restaurant space; renovation of the Blues Armory; and other items. This would be the largest economic development project in Richmond's history if it is reapproved by Richmond's City Counsel.

In 1816, a group of developers, including John G. Gamble, John Goddin, Peter Ralston and John Barfoot, sought to create what modern readers would call a "planned community." They chose a theme of heroes of naval battles against the British during the War of 1812 to name the community's

SA ∨ 85
NAVY HILL

The Navy Hill neighborhood, named as a tribute to nearby naval victories during the War of 1812, was settled by German immigrants beginning in 1810. It became a vibrant African American community by the turn of the century. Navy Hill's distinctive character was embodied in the buildings here between North Third and Thirteenth Streets. Navy Hill School was the only Richmond public school to employ black teachers. Area landmarks included the Bill "Bojangles" Robinson home, Good Samaritan Society, Phyllis Wheatley YMCA, and numerous churches. The construction of Interstate 95 destroyed Navy Hill in the 1960s.

DEPARTMENT OF HISTORIC RESOURCES, 2000

Navy Hill marker in Richmond. Navy Hill marker SA-85 is at the intersection of East Jackson Street and North Fourth Street in Richmond, Virginia. *Photograph courtesy of M. Robinson.*

streets. The streets were to radiate from a central column, honoring their courage, but the growing economy that allowed for such speculation went bust. The area remained an underdeveloped satellite of the current Jackson Ward; it had a few scattered houses and was cut off from other settlements by several deep ravines. For the district's development to begin, foot bridges and carriage paths needed to be laid across these gullies. Once the mid-nineteenth-century progress began, the neighborhood spread out roughly between Third and Fifth Streets, north of Leigh Street. Its northward expansion is indeterminate, but it at least reaches Duval and Preston Streets and, perhaps, Shockoe Cemetery. Its boundaries depend on the era and individual memory.[121]

In 1822, the home of Right Reverend Richard Channing Moore was on Fifth Street. Bishop Moore had come to Richmond in 1814 to be rector of the Monumental Church and the Bishop of Virginia. He lived in the house on Fifth Street until his death in 1841.[122] The Navy Hill part of Fifth Street had a very definitive character due to the large number of Germans who built their homes there in the late 1850s. On Fourth Street, researchers find only Caspar Wendlinger, the builder of several houses on the 800 Block, but on Fifth Street, those who built houses that are still standing were the Emmenhausers, Rebmans, Krauses, Gassers and Hoyers. This is not surprising when we know that the first German church in Richmond, which was later called St. John's Lutheran, was built in 1847 on the east side of Fifth Street, just north of Jackson Street. After moving to Eighth and Marshall Streets in 1881, the congregation moved to Stuart Circle.

Even in the eighteenth century, Germans settled in Richmond (hence the names Ege and Sherer among the earliest property owners). But in the 1840s and 1850s, they started coming in great numbers. In 1844, for example, the ships *Licilla* and *Palos* arrived with 150 German farmers and mechanics. Samuel Mordecai was enthusiastic over both the number of skilled workmen

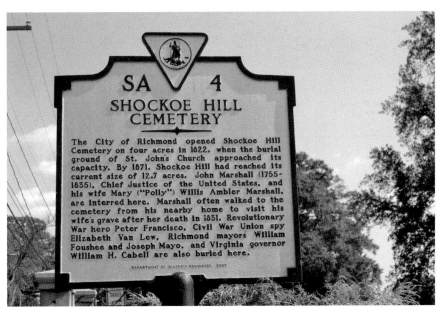

SA 4
SHOCKOE HILL
CEMETERY

The City of Richmond opened Shockoe Hill Cemetery on four acres in 1822, when the burial ground of St. John's Church approached its capacity. By 1871, Shockoe Hill had reached its current size of 12.7 acres. John Marshall (1755-1835), Chief Justice of the United States, and his wife Mary ("Polly") Willis Ambler Marshall, are interred here. Marshall often walked to the cemetery from his nearby home to visit his wife's grave after her death in 1831. Revolutionary War hero Peter Francisco, Civil War Union spy Elizabeth Van Lew, Richmond mayors William Foushee and Joseph Mayo, and Virginia governor William H. Cabell are also buried here.

DEPARTMENT OF HISTORIC RESOURCES 2007

Above: Shockoe Hill Cemetery (built in 1802) contains the graves of many historical figures, including Chief Justice John Marshall, on twenty-three acres. *Photograph courtesy of M. Robinson.*

Right: Statue of Bill "Bo" Bojangles, located on the Triangle at North Adams Street, East Leigh Street and Chamberlayne Parkway. *Photograph courtesy of M. Robinson and www.richmond.com.*

and the gaiety they contributed to Richmond. St. John's, Bethlehem Lutheran and St. Mary's Roman Catholic Churches were founded in the wake of this mass immigration. The chief centers where the newly arrived Germans settled were Union Hill and, to a greater extent, North Fifth, Third and Second Streets.

During the 1850s, the suburb on Navy Hill grew by leaps and bounds. On April 25, 1859, the *Dispatch* wrote:

> *Fifth Street, North of Leigh, is improving so rapidly that Navy Hill begins to present the appearance of a neat little village. A large number of pretty residences have sprung up in that section within a short time, and many others will be put up at once if the city would only bridge the gully so as to make a carriage way to the settlement.*

The house on the northern end of Fifth Street showed considerably more architectural variety than those on Fourth Street—probably because more were built to be occupied by their owners. But many have been altered, and few are noticeably attractive. An exception to this is No. 710, which was built by Charles C. Ellett in 1855, but it looks like a house that was built much earlier. No. 747½ is a quaint house that is set back in the yard; it is more like an outbuilding than a residence. No. 715, while so distorted by alterations that one would never guess it was built in 1854, is noteworthy for its exquisite little iron balcony that is almost concealed between it and the house south of it.

Returning toward Clay, there is a handsome row that was erected just before the Civil War at 508–18 North Fifth Street. John T. Sublett, Charles C. Ellett and others built six imposing three-story houses, which, with their delicate street-level iron verandahs, are almost identical to the rowhouses near Third, Franklin, Tenth and Clay Streets, which were built around the same time. The row on Fifth Street is in wretched condition; no one has had the imagination to see what handsome apartments could be made here for families who want a Prestwood or Monroe Terrace.

In the 1850s, Richmond was a classic "walking city," with working-class residents living in close proximity to industry and commerce. Class defined neighborhoods more than race. The wealthy "lived high" in the neighborhoods such as Church Hill and Gamble's Hill, while free blacks, hired slaves and white working people tended to occupy the bottoms and industrial areas. Clusters of immigrants established churches and self-help organizations near Navy Hill.[123]

Richmond Amory in the 1900s on Marshall Street. *Courtesy of www.navyhillrva.com.*

All of Richmond could find inspiration on the Navy Hill Marker located at Fourth and Jackson Streets. It reads:

Love and memories never die as days roll on and years pass by. Deep in our hearts, memories are kept of the ones we loved and shall never forget.

"STONE BATTLES"

The Shockoe Hill Cats and Butcher Cats have moved their trysting grounds from the hill at the head of Governor's Street to Navy Hill, between Fourth and Seventh Streets, where every Sunday afternoon, the whole neighborhood is grievously annoyed by the hideous yells and general misconduct of the boys engaged in these outrages. The police have not, of late, extended their visits to the vicinity of the suburbs that have been referred to, but the people of Richmond trust they will perceive the propriety of doing so in future. Citizens were informed that an infant was struck by a missile thrown by one of the belligerents last Sunday and was nearly killed.[124]

"ROCK BATTLE"

From time immemorial, the boys in Adams Valley (popularly known as Butchertown) and those residing on the north side of Shockoe Hill, have engaged, every successive summer, in "rock battles," rallying under the distinctive titles of Butcher Cats and Hill Cats. Within the last few years, the majority of these respectable white boys (among the former) have so far been convinced of the discreditable character of these conflicts as to leave them chiefly to (the African American) lads on their side, though a goodly number, influenced by the excitement of the mimic warfare, have participated in the "battles," which have taken place within the past few weeks.

Last Sunday afternoon, the contending parties waged a fierce contest on Navy Hill, about one hundred boys being engaged on each side. Stones and other missiles flew as thick, almost, as the Minnie balls at the Battle of Manassas, and it is wonderful that some of the belligerents were not maimed or seriously hurt. The progress of the fight was fortunately arrested by the timely arrival of officers Chalkley, Seal, Davis, Quarles, and Crone in one direction and officers Pleasants, Perria and others in an opposite direction.

At the sight of the police, the boys fled the field, but all of them did not make their escape. Six white boys and ten "negro" boys were captured and taken to the station house. The former was eventually bailed out, but the others were detained until next morning, when they were conducted to the presence of the mayor. The parents of the white boys were fined one dollar each, and admonished that a repetition of the offence would involve a heavier fine. "The 'negro' boys were ordered to be switched." The little darkies were ordered to be switched.[125]

In 1823, "a number of persons of colour residing in the City of Richmond" petitioned the state legislature for a church, noting "the number of free persons of colour and slaves has become very considerable." The petitioners requested "a law authorizing them to cause to be erected within this city, a house of public worship which may be called the Baptist African Church." It would be another eighteen years before the first African church was allowed to form in Richmond, and it was followed by three other Baptist churches that described themselves as African that were founded in the late antebellum era.[126] Job opportunities for free blacks were bleakest in the urban North, especially New England. Race riots racked numerous Northern cities throughout the antebellum era. Philadelphia, one of the most popular destinations for Richmond's free blacks, had at least five riots between 1826 and 1849.

Most Southern migrants moved to the urban North, as a segregated school promised more than no school at all. The opportunity to associate in churches and societies outside of the gaze of whites trumped the impositions of the Southern codes, and the ability to walk down the street without free papers or passes stood in sharp contrast to the Southern system. The North had its prejudices, but African American communities struggled against them in full public view—an impossibility in the South. For many, it was simply a matter of going where the system of slavery was dead, and many went.[127]

Catholic, Lutheran and Methodist churches anchored immigrant populations in areas such as Navy Hill, which was located just northwest of the central commercial district. Intersected by an area of free black settlements farther west around Leigh and Jackson Streets, a visitor to the Navy Hill neighborhood in 1858 could begin a tour on Fifth Street, above Jackson Street, at the German Lutheran Church, which was known to congregants as Saint John's. Richmonders walking through Union Hill, Navy Hill and other neighborhoods where Germans clustered could hear the regional dialects of Saxony, Hess and Hanover, among others. Charles Hennghausen remembered that he and his fellow German soldiers were still "conspicuous by [their] German speech" at the outbreak of the Civil War.

The solid houses of free black artisans, such as the homes of plasterer John Adams and seamstress Catherine Harris on West Leigh Street, shared the streets with the homes of white craftsmen and mechanics in a neighborhood bordering Navy Hill.[128] Later, Jackson Ward encompassed the old neighborhood of Navy Hill and the areas of free black settlement around Ebenezer Baptist Church. African Americans used their new freedom to reconstruct their families, which had been dispersed in the antebellum black diaspora. Black militias protected the African American community and served as another way to enter the public discourse on citizenship. African American militias marched to Capitol Square on the first Emancipation Day in 1866; it was held on April 3—the day Richmond fell to Union forces with regiments of the United States Colored Troops in the vanguard. Well aware of the symbolic importance of Capitol Square, from which they had been excluded by antebellum law, black citizens and soldiers carried their celebration into the symbolic heart of the Virginia capital.[129]

In Jackson Ward, a black-majority ward of post-1870 in Richmond, they gerrymandered, but blacks patronized and voted for white saloonkeepers and grocers in strong biracial alliances, reflecting the mixed population of the district. The ward encompassed the old neighborhood of Navy Hill and the areas of free black settlement around Ebenezer Baptist Church.[130]

SHOCKOE HILL

Shockoe Hill is one of several hills where much of the oldest portion of the city of Richmond, Virginia, was built. It extends north from the downtown area for about a mile, including where the state capitol complex sits, to a point where the hill falls off sharply to the winding path of Shockoe Creek. Today, Interstate 95 bisects the hill, separating the highly urbanized downtown portion from the more residential northern portion. There is a portion of Shockoe Hill on Main Street that has chiefly been given over to banks, offices and other businesses. However, the Richmond Capitol is the main building that belongs to the "upper tendon" of Shockoe Hill at Capital Square.

In the early 1800s, wooden buildings gave way to brick; in the 1840s, these were either torn down or were altered by granite or iron fronts. In the 1830s, the Falling Gardens Building on Main Street was the headquarters of the *Southern Literary Messenger* during the editorship of Edgar Allan Poe. Since banks had first been introduced to Richmond, this section has remained the center of the financial district.

Near the northern edge of Shockoe Hill are two important cemeteries. Shockoe Hill Cemetery is the burial place of Chief Justice John Marshall, American Revolutionary war hero Peter Francisco, Union spy Elizabeth Van Lew and many other notable figures. It also is the resting place of many Confederate soldiers. Hundreds of deceased Union prisoners of war were buried in less desirable land across the street to the east before being moved after the war. The Hebrew Cemetery of Richmond, which was founded in 1816, contains what is reputed to be the largest Jewish military burial ground in the world outside of Tel Aviv. Many of Richmond's Jewish elite, including William Thalhimer, founder of the Thalhimers Department Store, can be found there. Next to the Hebrew Cemetery is the Almshouse Building, which was built in 1860 as the city poor house, saw service as an American Civil War hospital and, in 1865, briefly served as the home of the Virginia Military Institute Corps of Cadets. Many Confederate soldiers who were buried in the two cemeteries died while hospitalized in that building.

In addition to these cemeteries, an unacknowledged African burial ground for slaves and free blacks known as Potter's Field is located on the corner of Hospital and Fifth Streets, directly east of the Hebrew cemetery. This cemetery originally comprised one acre for free people of color and one acre for slaves. This burial ground was established in 1816 by the City of Richmond and expanded over time. This land, however, contains nothing

A view of Shockoe Hill from Church Hill. *Photograph courtesy of M. Robinson and www. sperityventures.com.*

White House of the Confederacy, built in 1818 for Dr. Brockenbrough. It was the executive mansion for Jefferson Davis. *Photograph courtesy of M. Robinson.*

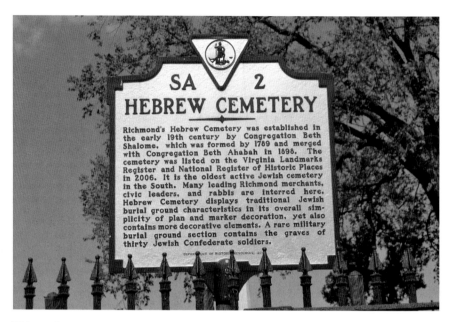

SA 2

HEBREW CEMETERY

Richmond's Hebrew Cemetery was established in the early 19th century by Congregation Beth Shalome, which was formed by 1789 and merged with Congregation Beth Ahabah in 1898. The cemetery was listed on the Virginia Landmarks Register and National Register of Historic Places in 2006. It is the oldest active Jewish cemetery in the South. Many leading Richmond merchants, civic leaders, and rabbis are interred here. Hebrew Cemetery displays traditional Jewish burial ground characteristics in its overall simplicity of plan and marker decoration, yet also contains more decorative elements. A rare military burial ground section contains the graves of thirty Jewish Confederate soldiers.

Hebrew Cemetery (built in 1816) contains the graves of thirty Jewish Confederate soldiers. At the time, it was one of only two military cemeteries in the United States. *Photograph courtesy of M. Robinson.*

on its surface that would cause it to be visibly recognizable as a cemetery today. It is believed that, between 1800 and 1865, an estimated 300,000 to 350,000 slaves were processed through the Shockoe Bottom Slave Auction Blocks in Richmond on their way to the Deep South. Shockoe Bottom also served as a burial ground for thousands of Africans who had not survived the journey or who had died shortly after their entry into America. In one of the more creative and dangerous escapes by a slave in the mid-1800s, Henry "Box" Brown, with the help of a sympathetic white shoemaker, Samuel Smith, had himself nailed into a two-by-three-foot box labelled "dry goods" before being loaded onto a northbound train from Richmond to freedom in Philadelphia, Pennsylvania.

Shockoe was named in the 1730 Tobacco Inspection Act as the site of a tobacco inspection warehouse on land owned by William Byrd II. Shockoe Bottom continued to develop in the late eighteenth century following the move of the state capital to Richmond, which was aided by the construction of Mayo's bridge in 1788 across the James River (it was ultimately succeeded by the replacement of the modern Fourteenth Street Bridge) and the siting of key tobacco industry structures, such as the public warehouse, tobacco scales and the federal customs house in or near the district.

Shockoe Bottom was also home to several historic sites and buildings, including the Edgar Allan Poe's home and Museum and the Mason's Hall, which was built between 1785 and 1787. Throughout the nineteenth century, Shockoe Bottom was the center of Richmond's commerce, with ships pulling into port from the James River. Goods from these ships were warehoused and traded in Shockoe Valley. Between the late seventeenth century and the end of the American Civil War in 1865, the area played a major role in the history of slavery in the United States, as it served as the second largest slave trading center in the country—second to New Orleans. Profits from the trade in human beings fueled the creation of wealth for southern whites and drove the economy in Richmond. This led Fifteenth Street to be known as Wall Street during the antebellum period, and the surrounding blocks were home to more than sixty-nine slave dealers and auction houses.

In 2006, archaeological excavations were started on the former site of Lumpkin's jail. Nearby is the African American Burial Ground, which was long used as a commercial parking lot (most recently, it was used by Virginia Commonwealth University, a state institution). It was reclaimed in 2011 after a decade-long community organizing campaign, and today, it is a memorial park.

On the eve of the fall of Richmond to the Union army in April 1865, evacuations of Confederate forces were ordered to set fire to the city's tobacco warehouses. The fires spread and completely destroyed Shockoe

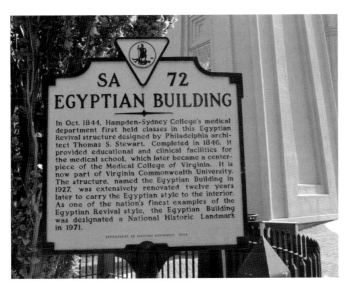

Egyptian building plaque, October 1844. The building originally housed Hampton-Sydney College medical department's classes; it is now used for Virginia Commonwealth University medical classes. *Photograph courtesy of M. Robinson.*

A front view of the Egyptian building, which was built in October 1844 at what was then the Hampton-Sydney College Medical Department. *Photograph courtesy of M. Robinson.*

Slip and several other districts. The district was quickly rebuilt in the late 1860s so that it flourished further in the 1870s and formed much of its present historic building stock.

Many of the buildings were constructed during the rebuilding that followed the evacuation fire of 1865 in a commercial variant of the Italianate style, including a 1909 fountain that was dedicated to "one who loved animals." The buildings in the district, which historically housed a variety of offices and wholesale and retail establishments, are now primarily restaurants, shops, offices and apartments. It warehoused many of the city's goods—but mostly tobacco.

The district began declining in the 1920s, as other areas of the city rose in prominence with the advent of the automobile. Numerous structures were demolished and cleared, including (in the 1950s), the Tobacco Exchange, which had been at the heart of the district, moved from Tobacco Row in the 1980s. The area was home to many of the country's largest tobacco companies.

The Confederate capital took over the state capital when it moved from Montgomery, Alabama, in 1861 and continued in Richmond until 1865, at the end of the Civil War. After the Civil War, the capital's congress met at Lynchburg for only five days before moving back to Richmond.

CHURCH HILL

Church Hill is known as the St. John's Church Historic District. This district encompasses the original land plat of the city of Richmond. Church Hill is the eastern terminus of Broad Street, a major east-west thoroughfare in the Richmond metropolitan area. The name Church Hill is often used to describe both the specific historic district and the larger general area in the East End that encompasses other neighborhoods, such as Union Hill, Chimborazo, Fairmount, Peter Paul, Woodville, et cetera.

Today, Church Hill is still, by far, the most attractive of Richmond's old neighborhoods. Its proportion of antebellum houses is higher than in any neighborhood of comparable size. The effect of the picturesque buildings, the beautiful churchyard grounds surrounding St. John's and the spire of old Trinity give Church Hill a charm that one cannot find in any other Richmond building, with the exception of maybe the capitol.

Church Hill is known for Chimborazo Park, where the largest American Civil War hospital was located. It is also known as the site of Virginia's second revolutionary convention, where Patrick Henry gave his famous "Give Me Liberty or Give Me Death" speech in St. John's Episcopal Church in 1775.

The Publick Market was established by the Virginia General Assembly in 1779. It was part of the deal when the state transferred the capital

Chimborazo Hospital (1861–65). Dr. McCaw developed the Confederate military hospital that served more than seventy-six thousand patients. *Photograph courtesy of M. Robinson.*

Battle of Bloody Run (1656). Colonel Hills and Chief Totopopotomoy fought with the Rickohockans and were killed. *Photograph courtesy of M. Robinson.*

from Williamsburg to Richmond. At the time, Seventeenth Street was known as First Street, hence the "First Market" moniker. Main Street was also the main road that connected Williamsburg and Richmond. It was an important thoroughfare, and it placed the First Market in a perfect location for trading. In the beginning, it was simply an open shed, with some wooden posts and a roof.

St Johns Church

1741

Henrico Parish Church (established in 1611) moved to Richmond in 1741 and was housed in what is now the Church Hill neighborhood, on land that was donated by William Byrd II. Byrd also donated timber to build the church and wood to fire the kiln for the foundation bricks. Henrico's county seat was also moved from Varina to Richmond in 1752. The county offices were moved to a building that is still extant at present-day Twenty-Second and Main Streets, where it operated until the 1970s.

The builder of the new church was Colonel Richard Randolph (1686–1748), the great-uncle of Thomas Jefferson. The original church building was completed on June 10, 1741, on the hill that was then called Indian Town. It remains as the transept of the current church, built along east-west lines. In 1772, a forty-foot-square extension was added to the northern side, orienting the church toward the south, and the altar was moved to that end. The church's casual names were the Church, the Old Church, the Church on Richmond Hill and, finally, St. John's Church.

The churchyard has undergone many changes. The wooden fence that surrounded the lot in 1746 was replaced by a four-and-a-half-foot-high brick wall that was built around the perimeter in 1770. In 1799, the city purchased the two lots between the churchyard and Broad Street and enclosed the entire square with yet another brick wall. St. John's relinquished the burying ground after the city agreed to bear the expense of keeping up the entire churchyard, an arrangement that continues to work today.[131]

As business was revived with the arrival of the railroads and the accompanying expansion of the iron industry, several houses were added to Church Hill. Built before 1816, 2302 East Grace was the home of Hilary Baker, who later became the first treasurer of the Richmond and Fredericksburg Railroad.[132] There was a tendency for two friends or partners to build pairs of houses together. Until just before the Civil War, nearly all of the houses built on Church Hill were made of brick.

By 1849, the hill still had only one church: St. John's. Over one hundred similar frame churches existed in Virginia before the American Revolution, but only four are still standing today. One of these is the Old Chapel Church in Franklin County, Virginia.

Wickham-Valentine House. The Wickham family lived here in 1790. *Photograph courtesy of M. Robinson.*

SECOND VIRGINIA CONVENTION

The Virginia colonial legislative assembly, the house of burgesses, was dismissed by the royal governor due to tensions that led up to the American Revolutionary War. The burgesses met as a provisional government in the First Virginia Convention in Williamsburg. Since the governor had loyalist forces in the vicinity of the capital of Williamsburg, it was decided to hold the next convention in Richmond. On March 23, 1775, the Second Virginia Convention was opened at the church. The president of the convention was Peyton Randolph, who was also the speaker of the house of burgesses.

The Reverend Miles Selden was the rector of St. John's Church at the time, and when the convention assembled, he was chosen as the chaplain. Selden was popularly referred to as the Patriot Parson. Among the 120 delegates at the convention were Thomas Jefferson and George Washington. Other notable delegates were Benjamin Harrison V, Thomas Mann Randolph, Richard Bland, Richard Henry Lee and Francis Lightfoot Lee. Debate centered on the perceived need to raise a militia to resist the British government's encroachments on civil rights under King George III. Patrick Henry, a delegate from Hanover County, rose in support of such a militia,

William H. Grant House, 1856. Grant bought the property from John Wickham. It was also kown as Sheltering Arms Hospital from 1892 to 1965. *Photograph courtesy of M. Robinson.*

and with his fiery speech (concluding with the words "give me liberty or give me death!"), he swayed the vote.

Under a resolution offered by Richard Henry Lee, the house of burgesses, on May 15, 1776, resolved that "the delegates appointed to represent this colony in general congress be instructed to propose to that respectable body to declare the united colonies free and independent states." It is notable that the Second Virginia Convention authorized Baptist chaplains to minister to soldiers, as this was an important step toward freedom of religion in what became the commonwealth of Virginia. Baptists and Methodists had been influential in Virginia during and after the Great Awakening, and many of the state's common people had already become affiliated with Baptist and Methodist congregations. After the war, the Anglican Church was disestablished, and the Episcopal Church of the United States was organized.

Third Virginia Convention

The Third Virginia Convention was held at St. John's Church on July 17, 1775, to organize the troops and the war effort of Virginia. George Washington of Fairfax had been appointed the head of the American army. The delegates acknowledged their debt to Patrick Henry, whose wisdom had already begun arming the colony, and he was named the first governor of Virginia.

American Revolutionary War

During the American Revolutionary War, in January 1781, General Benedict Arnold, the traitor who was then serving on the British side, quartered his troops in the church when Richmond was occupied. At the end of the Revolution, the Virginia government moved its capital from Williamsburg to Richmond. There, the general assembly, at its first session, passed an act that determined the character of Church Hill forever; the new capitol building would be built on Shockoe Hill, not Church Hill. Thus, Church Hill did not become the hub of the emerging metropolis; rather, it became a quiet residential community that was somewhat removed from the rest of the city.[133]

HISTORY OF RICHMOND HILL
(ON CHURCH HILL)[134]

There is anecdotal evidence that suggests Richmond Hill, the highest hill in Richmond, has been a place of prayer for several millennia. Native Americans confirmed this use of the hill when the land was still known as Tsenacomoco. The hill overlooks the Falls of the James River and faces the setting sun.

William Byrd II of Westover was granted the land by King James and commissioned Colonel William Mayo to lay out a city on Richmond Hill in 1737. The survey lines of Byrd's and Mayo's city still form the legal boundaries of the property of Richmond Hill. Colonel Richard Adams, a native of New Kent County, moved to Richmond Hill in 1769. At that time, Richmond was still largely undeveloped, a condition that prevailed until it was declared the capital of Virginia in 1779. Adams purchased a number of squares on the southeastern promontory of Church Hill. His first house was probably located on the north side of Grace Street, across from the present Richmond Hill.

Church Hill or Richmond in 1790, when the house was built. The second house, Monte Maria, was built in 1810. *Photograph courtesy of M. Robinson and the Department of Historic Resources, Richmond, Virginia.*

In the mid-1780s, soon after Richmond became the capital, Adams built an attractive mansion on the crest of Richmond Hill overlooking the James River and the Shockoe Valley. Adams was senior warden of the nearby St. John's Church; represented Henrico County in the house of burgesses, the house of delegates and the senate after independence; and he was one of the twelve founding members of the Common Council of Richmond. He later became its sixth mayor. Writing in his remarkable early history of Richmond, Samuel Mordecai described the prominence of Richard Adams and his descendants in the first half of the nineteenth century:

This hill is divided by little dells into a succession of spurs, forming a cluster of heights overlooking the river, the city and the surrounding country. The proprietor assigned to each of his sons and married daughters one of these prominences. The eldest son, Richard Adams, possessed the fine old family mansion, now Mr. Ellett's. John erected his mansion east of it, now Mrs. Van Lew's; William Marshall, who married a Miss Adams, built yet further east, and his house is now the center of a row, as it was once of an open square, on Franklin, Grace, Twenty-Sixth and Twenty-Seventh Streets.

Southeast of Mr. Marshall, another son-in-law, George W. Smith, placed his residence, a neat wooden building, on Franklin, Main, Twenty-Seventh and Twenty-Eighth [Streets]. This gentleman was governor of Virginia at the time that the theatre was burned and was one of the victims in consequence of his efforts to save others. Samuel G. Adams, the youngest of the sons, erected the building on the western slope of the hill, on Broad Street, now the Bellevue Hospital. The possessions of the Adams family in Richmond and elsewhere gave them a prospect of great wealth in the natural course of thing, but impelled by an enterprising spirit, the two younger brothers sought to hasten the event. The chapter on "Flush Times" gives the result.

George Nicolson, once mayor of the city (as was also Dr. John Adams), resided on one of the adjacent and most commanding heights overlooking the city and the surrounding country. The land west of it and south of Mr. Marshall's and Governor Smith's, embracing the slope of the hill, has recently been purchased by the city for a public square [now Libby Park]. Mr. Nicolson's residence was destroyed by fire some years ago. His descendants are among our worthy citizens.

Tradition holds that the elder Adams failed in his greatest ambition, which was to persuade his friend Thomas Jefferson to place the new state capitol on the hill where he and his family lived. Adams is said to never have spoken with Jefferson following that adverse decision.

In 1859, William Taylor acquired the house that Richard Adams Jr. had built for $6,500, and by 1860, he had enlarged it significantly, adding a second story, an enclosed cupola and two-story Italianate porches. In 1860, he sold the house for $20,000 to Richard A. Wilkins, a Virginian who had

Confederate Soldiers and Sailors Monument at Libby Hill Park. *Photograph courtesy of M. Robinson.*

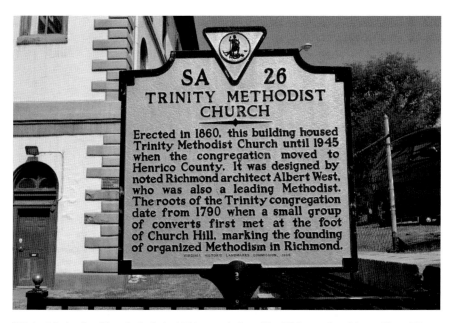

Trinity Methodist Church, built in 1860, was designed by Richmond architect Albert West. *Photograph courtesy of M. Robinson.*

been running a large sugar plantation in Louisiana and wished to return to Richmond to educate his children. Wilkins's young son, Benjamin Harrison Wilkins, often sat in the cupola over the next four years. He watched the smoke, and by its movement, he followed the seven days of battles when the Union attacked Confederate lines north of the city and were forced to move east and south around the city and across the James River. Mrs. Wilkins visited the hospitals throughout the city, bringing wounded friends to recuperate in her home. Soon after the war, the Wilkins family sold their Richmond Hill mansion to the Catholic bishop and moved to Tennessee. In the last decade of the century, the embittered son wrote an account of his early years entitled *War Boy* and told of the view from the cupola.

Church Hill is still, by far, the most attractive of Richmond's old neighborhoods.

Silkworm Farm Breeding Worms at Bellona

1837–1842

For a number of years, the Bellona property and buildings were vacant, and the question of whether the government could suggest financial support for the buildings and land arose many times. By 1837, however, it became clear that there was much more space in the Bellona buildings than was needed for its original purpose. When a Virginia civilian requested permission to lease the arsenal buildings, which were admittedly "almost useless to the government," the war department listened with interest. Thomas Mann Randolph of Tuckahoe, a half-brother of the governor, believed that "the climate and soil of middle America" were peculiarly adapted to "the culture of silk."[135] To test this theory, he wanted to plant mulberry trees and establish a cocoonery at Bellona. Permission was given, and Randolph moved in as the government's tenant.

Ambitious and able, Randolph was active in the political arena of his time; he served as a congressman, a governor of his state and as a member of the Virginia General Assembly. During the second war against England, he also took part in Wilkinson's St. Lawrence campaign of 1813 in defense of his native commonwealth. Randolph is interesting, however, not only because he shared the predicaments of the Virginia plantation aristocracy in the morning of its decline but also because of his relationship with one of the great men of his day. Soon after his marriage, he settled down at Edgehill Plantation in Albemarle County, near Monticello. From that time on, his life was so closely interwoven with that of his father-in-law that he has been remembered, when he is remembered at all, as Jefferson's son-in-law.[136]

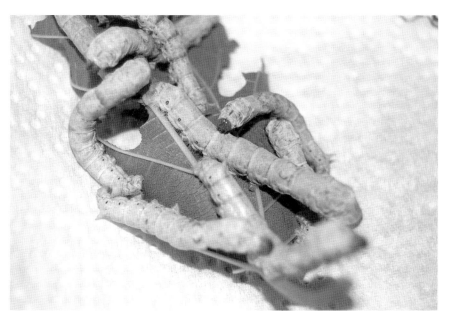

Mulberry leaves being eaten by the worms. *Courtesy of* www.suekayton.com.

Around this time, the people of every class in Chesterfield were engaged in one of the most widespread fantastic schemes that ever struck the nation—the *morus multicaulis*, or silk worm boom, which developed into a national mania. Elsewhere in the nation, the craze had started earlier, but when it belatedly struck Chesterfield, it found fertile soil. For ten years, the wild mania swept the Eastern Seaboard before the orgy of speculation ended, as most booms do, with a loud, sickening thud.

The idea, which originated in New England, was that the culture of silk would be comparatively easy if the proper food was supplied for the worms. The Chinese mulberry grown in France was their favorite. Before long, France was almost denuded of its mulberry trees, and the shoots brought to America were sold by the tens of thousands. When the craze reached Chesterfield, the trees were planted in every available space, including cemeteries. People mortgaged their homes to buy the trees and the worms. In the early days of the boom, the shoots were sold at $2 per one hundred, but the supply could not meet the demand, and process mounted like stocks on a bull market. Before the bubble was pricked, they were bringing $500 per one hundred, and some speculators rejoiced at getting a single choice root for $25.

At the height of the frenzy, it was widely proclaimed that in the not distant future, every farm would be a nursery for young trees, every house would have its cocoonery and two, three or four crops would be harvested yearly. The farmers' wives, when not engaged in feeding the worms, were to reel the silk and perhaps spin and twist it "until silk would become as cheap as cotton and every matron and maid rejoice in the possession of at least a dozen silk dresses." Dunlop, Moncure & Company, which later built and operated the now fire-gutted Dunlop Mills at the south foot of Mayo's Bridge, was among the earliest of the firms in this locality to deal in the morus multicaulis, and its first offering was for a modest twenty thousand trees, but a little later it was offering five hundred thousand buds. Silkworm eggs were advertised by the hundreds of thousands and even came in an assortment of colors.

In the late winter of 1837, Thomas Mann Randolph made a report to the general assembly on the value and importance of a state bounty for the culture of silk, and a laboratory was setup at Bellona Arsenal for the study and raising of mulberry trees and the manufacture of silk.[137] The following spring, Thomas Pleasants and Henry Clarke joined Randolph in advertising a nursery on the arsenal property and stated, "We are prepared to purchase cocoons and will be enabled to furnish the growers of silk with silkworm eggs of the most approved kind." They announced, "We have engaged an assistant who is thoroughly acquainted with the care of the worm in all its stages, feeding, et cetera, as well as with the structure of the newest and most approved cocooneries; making silk reels and realign the silk."

Thomas Jefferson had experimented with mulberry trees at Monticello, and sericulture (silk farming) had been tried, with some success, in northern states.[138] Landowners were beguiled with predictions that an acre of trees would yield between $200 and $500. The usually reliable *Richmond Enquirer* wrote of yields of up to $1,000 per acre. Large and small fell for the propaganda, and the Mechanics Manufacturing Company at Swift Creek was given authority in its charter to cultivate mulberry trees and raise silkworms.

Along with the speculation in trees and eggs came kindred lines. There were magazines devoted to silk culture; so-called "experts" were retained at large salaries, lectures spread a lot of misinformation and everybody talked silk. A Glasgow merchant offered to build a $150,000 plant in Virginia, provided that the legislature would make certain concessions, which were promptly given. The Bellona Arsenal's proprietors were strong bidders for this project.

The mulberry trees (at Bellona) flourished quickly, the squirming worms were set to work, and in due time, heaps and heaps of cocoons were ready for the next important step—but it was not as simple as it had seemed. Fingers accustomed to working in the fields, forests and mines were not adapted to the delicate handling of the gossamer-like threads. Machines for doing the work were patented but were not easy to acquire or to operate despite optimistic claims. One advertiser offered a "most simple, easy, expeditious, beautiful and economical machine for spooling and reeling the raw material from the cocoons and for twisting and making sewing silk" for thirty-five dollars. Any blacksmith or carpenter, he asserted, could keep the machine in repair. He claimed that the machine could spool 332,840 yards of silk thread in ten hours. Some Chesterfield attics still house the contraptions.

Then, this undertaking became the ultimate disillusionment. Many of the trees didn't prove as hardy as had been promised; when harvested, many of the cocoons were found to be defective, probably due to ignorance in their culture and handling. Although entire families took turns unravelling the cocoons, few had the ability, the patience or the space in their homes for the various steps in the operation. Individuals also had lost their trees to improper sericulture, worms simmered down to a trickle and speculators duped their supplies at rapidly dwindling prices. Worms and eggs took a tumble as well, and within a year or two, the bubble burst, leaving a long trail of debt behind it.[139]

In the late winter of 1837, Thomas Mann Randolph made a report to the general assembly on the value and importance of a state bounty for the culture of silk, and a laboratory was set up at Bellona Arsenal for the study and raising of mulberry trees and the manufacture of silk. The "zealous" but "prudent" Sergeant McArthur remained on the scene to watch over the public property and to superintend the continuing storage of Major Clarke's cannons. Friction soon developed between him and the new tenant, as the latter found it "extremely irksome" to be "placed in subordination" to the sergeant. Randolph was also upset by the occasional explosions at the nearby foundry. "The walls and enclosures were disfigured and materially mutilated," he reported, and human life was placed in great jeopardy. Nonetheless, he remained at his chosen post of danger for almost three years.

Near the end of that period, he announced that "the laboratory for the culture of silk" would soon be "crowned with entire success." Unfortunately, however, he found himself forced by "other and extraneous duties" to abandon the enterprise. Therefore, in 1840, he departed from Bellona after recommending that his friend and partner, Thomas S. Pleasants Jr. of Goochland County, should be allowed to continue the project in his stead. It soon appeared, however, that Randolph's predictions of success had been overly optimistic. In early 1842, "the experiment to raise silk, having faded," Pleasants abandoned the enterprise. "He cut down the mulberry trees at Bellona, planted corn in the walled quadrangle and installed pens for hogs in the lower rooms of the tenements." He neglected to clean the upper apartments; they were in "a very filthy condition, with mulberry brush and dead worms." Sergeant McArthur reported all this to his superiors, and Pleasants, in due course, departed. By this time, the buildings' exteriors were also showing visible signs of neglect, and one of them, the old barracks, had been pulled down.

With the silk adventure unsuccessful at Bellona, how would Archer begin his adventure in convincing the United States to lease his property for use in the upcoming Civil War?

Epilogue:
Richmond's Civil War Events

1861–1865

Confederate's Laboratory on Brown's Island

Brown's Island is an artificial continental island on the James River formed by the Haxall Canal. Brown's Island was formed in 1789 with the beginnings of the Haxall Canal. The Haxall Canal, which forms what is now Brown's Island at the foot of Seventh Street, was first built by David Ross as Overton's Canal and later became Ross's Mill Road. Ross's Mill was at the south end of Thirteenth Street. The island's first settler, for whom it was named, was Elijah Brown. He acquired the land in 1826. A later owner named Neilson tried to rename the island Neilson's Island, but it did not last.

During the American Civil War, the island was the home of the Confederate States Laboratory. The Confederate laboratory produced ammunition, friction primers, percussion caps and other ordnance for the Confederate war effort. The laboratory, which was just a mound of dirt, had been established by Captain Wesley Smith in early 1861. Smith hired a small number of workers, trained them and hired more as necessary. It is thought that the mostly female workers, who were aged between nine and twenty, turned out an average of 1,200 cartridges a day.

The Confederate States Laboratory department that produced munitions was located on Brown's Island, just south of the arsenal. Out of a total of about six hundred workers, the laboratory employed three hundred to four hundred young women daily in munitions production. In addition to the

Two portable pontoon bridges facing west, over the James River, just east of Gambles Hill, in the 1860s. *Courtesy of the Library of Congress.*

guns produced at the arsenal, an extremely efficient process was developed for producing percussion caps that enabled them to produce three hundred thousand caps a day with a team of only eight people. The finished arms and munitions were issued from the arsenal.

Most workers made about one or two dollars a day, depending on their skill level and gender. There were a number of accidents at the arsenal and laboratory, but the most serious occurred on a Friday the thirteenth in 1863, when a building housing Laboratory Department 6 exploded, killing forty-five and injuring twenty-three, again, mostly young women. The accident occurred while a worker, Mary Ryan, was disassembling a friction primer too forcefully; it exploded, igniting loose power on the same table and triggering a much larger explosion. Ryan had hit the board off of the table three times trying to free the primer, which blew her up to the ceiling. Numerous other girls were also filling cartridges and breaking up condemned ones, which added to the danger.

A witness recalled that the room was "blown into a complete wreck, the roof lifted off, and the walls dashed out, the ruins falling upon the occupants." As the dust settled, "the most heart-rending lamentations and cries…from sufferers rendered delirious from suffering and terror." From an officer connected with the laboratory, they learned that the department destroyed was under the charge of Mr. McCarthy, superintendent. In that department, condemned cartridges were broken by the girls who distributed the bullets into one receptacle and the powder into another. It is surmised that a percussion cap containing fulminating ingredients got mixed in with the powder and created an explosion.

Top: Clarke's single lunette window in the state capitol. *Courtesy of Charles Rose Real Estate.*

Bottom: RF&P Railroad notice in 1865. *Courtesy of the Library of Congress.*

As word of the accident made its way through the city, a "tide of people" gathered at the footbridge leading to Brown's Island. One account noted that "mothers rushed about, throwing themselves upon the corpses of the dead and the persons of the wounded." A newspaper article noted, "Some had an arm or a leg divested of flesh and skin, others were bleeding with wounds received from the falling timbers or in the violent concussions against the floor and ceiling which ensued." The treatment of burns at the time was often ineffective and painful. Every day for the next eleven days, one of the victims died. Many of the girls, including Mary Ryan, were buried in Richmond's historic Hollywood Cemetery.

For a city that already knew and understood suffering during wartime, this was a new level of tragedy for Richmond. The laboratory buildings were quickly rebuilt and resumed production.[140]

RICHMOND ARSENAL
(VIRGINIA MANUFACTORY OF ARMS)

The Virginia Manufactory of Arms was first built and in operation in 1785; however, it ended operations in 1820. When the Civil War began in 1861, its name was changed to the Richmond Arsenal, and the arms plant began producing superior warfare equipment again. The Richmond Arsenal was established after the Confederate government's move to Richmond from Montgomery, Alabama, in May 1861. The James River front proved to be a natural location, as it was between the river and the Kanawha Canal.

The two-story brick Virginia State Armory, Byrd Island, Brown's Island and, of course, the great Tredegar Iron Works were all converted into Confederate ordnance-making facilities. The Virginia State Armory became known as the Confederate State Armory after Virginia seceded. Today, little physical evidence of the structure can be found in Richmond. The ordnance department, armory, arsenal, laboratory and all other facilities were completely destroyed in the fiery conflagration that accompanied the Confederate evacuation of Richmond in April 1865.

A great number of cavalry troopers' and officers' equipment was manufactured at Clarksville until early spring 1863, when the superintendent of armories at the Richmond Arsenal, Major Downer, began seeking outside contracts with commercial suppliers for the majority of his troops' equipment. Throughout the war, the lion's share

A Front View of the Penitentiary at Richmond, a painting by the artist Woodford, 1830. *Courtesy of the Library of Congress.*

of finished horse equipment and manufacturing resources that were imported by the bureau from abroad went to the Richmond Arsenal. The Clarksville Ordnance Harness Shop was the only source of artillery harnesses and saddlery for the Richmond Arsenal and the Army of Northern Virginia. In general, over the course of the four-year struggle, a herculean effort was undertaken to organize and build up the widely scattered commercial establishments of the South's agrarian economy into some semblance of an effective military industrial complex. These proved to be remarkably successful.[141]

As we have seen, at the beginning of the Civil War, the Confederate States had very few improved small arms, no powder mills of any importance, very few modern cannons and only small arsenals that had been captured from the federal government. There was almost an entire lack of other ordnance stores—no saddles or bridles, no artillery harnesses, no accouterments and very few of the minor articles that were required to equip an army. In the arsenals that were captured from the federal government, there were about 120,000 muskets of old types, and 12,000 to 15,000 rifles. In addition to these, the states had a few muskets, bringing the total available supply of small arms for infantry up to about 150,000. With this handicap, the states entered the greatest war in American history.

The first step was to organize an ordnance department. Colonial Gorgas, a graduate of the U.S. Military Academy, was appointed chief of ordnance around the end of February 1861. The department immediately sent out purchasing officers. With Richmond serving as the seat of the Confederate government in Richmond, Colonial Gorgas proceeded to organize the center of activity of the ordnance department. There were four main sources of supply: arms on hand, those captured from the Union, those manufactured in the Confederacy and those imported from abroad. The principal dependence was on the importations at first, but the stringency of the Union blockade rendered it imperative that every effort be made to increase the domestic manufacture of all kinds of ordnance and ordnance stores. Special machinery was made in England and shipped, but it did not reach its destination in time for use. A large installment that included a powerful pair of engines had reached Bermuda when blockade running practically came to an end near the end of the war.

The arms work was scattered among a number of available places throughout the South, but transportation was a problem. However, the Confederacy took possession of them, and various temporary ordnance works grew up around existing foundries, machine shops and railroad repair shops. The chief localities that were used were in Richmond, Virginia, and eleven other cities.

Heavy artillery at the beginning of the war was manufactured only at Richmond's Tredegar Iron Works. With the difficulties and the constantly increasing pressure for immediate results, the Confederate Ordnance Department was able to boast of some useful new experiments and some improvements. One of the most notable of these was the method of steaming the mixed, moistened materials for gunpowder just before incorporation in the cylinder mills, which was invented and brought into use by Colonel Rains.[142] It greatly increased the capacity of the mills for work and improved the quality of the powder.[143]

Between July 1, 1861, and January 1, 1865, the Richmond Arsenal issued 341 Columbiads and siege-guns, 1,306 field pieces, 921,441 rounds of artillery ammunition, 323,231 infantry arms, 34,067 cavalry carbines, 6,074 pistols and nearly 72,500,000 rounds of small arms. It has been assumed that the Richmond Arsenal had issued a half of all Confederate troops' weapons. Considering the general lack of previous experience in ordnance matters, the personnel of these corps, both at the arsenals and in the field, deserved great praise for intelligence, zeal and efficiency.[144]

THE RICHMOND ARMORY IN PRODUCTION FOR THE CONFEDERACY

The arms produced in Richmond by the State of Virginia and the Confederate States of America originated from the Harpers Ferry Armory. Harpers Ferry, which apparently began to produce arms around 1800, ended production in 1861, when Lieutenant Roger Jones, who was in command of the small body of U.S. troops there in the face of advancing Virginia forces, set fire to the arsenal and the armory buildings to prevent their capture. The Virginians, aided by local citizenry and the employees of the armory, worked to put out the fire but were unable to save some sixteen thousand to seventeen thousand finished rifles and muskets that were destroyed along with the arsenal building and the carpentry shop. The machinery and material preserved from destruction was gradually boxed and then sent to Winchester; from there, it traveled by wagon to Strasburg, where it was placed on the Manassas Gap Railroad for the final leg of the journey to Richmond.

It is perhaps ironic that the death of the Harpers Ferry Armory meant the rebirth of the Virginia Manufactory. The Virginia Manufactory, which had last produced arms in 1821, became the Virginia State Armory and then the Richmond Armory; it was the new home for the equipment taken from Harpers Ferry. The Richmond Armory rifled muskets can be easily identified by their humpback lock plates that were made from forgings and

Richmond Arsenal ruins with Brown's Island in the background in 1865. *Courtesy of the Library of Congress.*

dyes from the U.S. Model 1855 Maynard tape primer lock plates that were captured at Harpers Ferry. The Model 1855 lock was made to be milled out for the use of paper primers. Richmond left the locks intact and simply used the standard percussion caps directly on the nipple.

The production report from January 1, 1864, indicates that, for the preceding two years, a total of 23,381 Model 1855 rifle muskets were produced in Richmond, along with 1,225 Model 1842 muskets (probably assembled from captured parts) and 2,764 rifle carbines. Of course, the total expectation could never be realized, as the city of Richmond was evacuated in 1865, and the buildings comprising the armory were gutted by a fire on the morning of April 3, 1865. It may be roughly assumed that the total rifle musket production was between 30,000 to 35,000 and carbine production was somewhat less than 10,000, perhaps as little as half that.

The Confederacy hoped to renew production at some other location, as evidenced by the fact that when the buildings burned, the contents had apparently already been removed. Finally, the equipment taken from Harpers Ferry to Richmond Armory included:

Arms Produced: The Richmond Armory produced four categories of weapons: the rifle, the musket, the carbine and the musketoon.

The Rifle Musket: The first weapons produced after the machinery arrived at Richmond probably used the stocks, mountings and even barrels captured at Harpers Ferry. The date 1861 appears on the rear of the hammer and the words "Richmond, Va." in block letters appear at the front of the plate. Very few Richmond muskets from 1861 and 1862 have the letters "JB" stamped into the rear of the trigger guard plate. Production of this same rifle musket continued unchanged through 1863 and 1864; the only distinguishable difference was the dating on the lock plate. The barrel length was also reduced to thirty-three inches, and the stock was reduced to a two-banded model. The front sight was also changed to a larger base.

The Musketoon: The records show a musketoon, which is described as having been designed especially for naval usage to permit easier handling, with a barrel cut to a thirty-inch length, and for more rapid loading on ship service, where long range accuracy was not so important.

Ruins of the Richmond Arsenal following its destruction in April 1865. *Courtesy of* The Photographic History of the Civil War, *R.S. Lanier, 1911.*

The Carbine: The carbine production of the Richmond Armory has no exact parallel in the United States' pattern of producing arms. The musketoon represents the first design for use by mounted troops, and it was in production until 1863, when the shorter rifled version was substituted, as it was easier to produce.

Bayonets: The appearance of the bayonet as it was produced at Richmond continues to be debated. It describes the bayonet as being only different in length from the 1855 blade.

Gun Tool: This was the tool for the disassembly of the weapon, and it was especially used for the removal of the nipple in a percussion piece, which was indispensable to the soldier. The Richmond Armory was completely gutted by a fire that was started by the Union forces on April 3, 1865.

ARCHER'S BELLONA ARSENAL AND FOUNDRY

Later documents leave no doubt that Junius L. Archer was directly in charge of foundry operations. Land Tax records list that the estate of John Clarke, from 1814 to 1859, was owned by Julius L. Archer. Archer came into control of the Bellona Foundry and Boring Mill through outright purchase. As the outcome of a court case in 1851, the property was to be sold at auction, and the estate was to be divided between the three daughters of John Clarke. Junius L. Archer purchased the property and was granted possession in 1861.[145]

Archer contracted with an important foundry in Southwest Virginia for gun metal. Graham had furnished the Bellona Foundry with gun iron during

Bellona Main Arsenal No. 1 with only the remaining walls visible in 1865. *Courtesy of Charles Rose Real Estate.*

the late 1850s and reputedly produced a high-quality metal. In April 1861, approximately fifty eight-inch Columbias were cast at Bellona Foundry, as the federal government had been detained by Virginia Authorities and were available for service. The South came into its greatest store of heavy ordnance on April 21, 1861, when Virginia troops occupied the Gasport Navy Yard at Norfolk.[146]

When the Civil War began in 1861, Virginia had fourteen charcoal iron furnaces in operation; twenty-two others had been temporarily shut down. If Virginia's demand for pig iron for munitions and machinery was not met, closed furnaces would have to be reopened and new ones would have to be built. During the war, the western counties of Virginia seceded from Virginia to become West Virginia, which remained loyal to the Union. Because of its proximity to West Virginia, the Shenandoah Valley was invaded by Union forces. The valley's pig iron furnaces and forges that furnished the Confederacy with weapons and other strategic materials became a prime target for destruction by the Union forces.[147]

At the outbreak of the war, Confederate president Jefferson Davis remembered Bellona Arsenal and the cannon foundry nearby and leased the property to the Confederacy from General Cocke. President Davis foresaw the probability of difficulties in importing materials because of blockades, so he made haste in buying firepower and balls in Europe and he had them shipped to southern ports. Much of this ammunition was shipped overland to Richmond and was stored at Bellona.[148] Pig iron from the Liberty Furnace was recovered from the James River around Bellona Foundry some years ago. Liberty Furnace operated in Shenandoah County between 1821 and 1905 and had a production run of 387 tons recorded in a twenty-week season. When riverine transport was used from Liberty Furnace, the pig iron traveled through the Potomac River's drainage, down the C&O Canal to Georgetown and thence down the Chesapeake Bay, through Hampton Roads, up the James River to Richmond and onto bateaux to Bellona. Water shipping in the nineteenth century seems to have been the preferred mode of transportation due to the high rate charged for waggonage.[149]

Later in 1861, Virginia seceded from the Union, and Dr. Archer set his foundry to work manufacturing ordnance for the Confederacy. For the first two years of the war, Archer operated his shops as a private individual, supplying guns to the government in Richmond on contract. When the convention was deliberating, the disposition of fifty heavy Columbiads manufactured for the U.S. government at the Bellona Foundry by Dr. Junius L. Archer were being decided. The shipment of the Columbiads was causing a stir; both the North and South brought the duel to Richmond. The huge weapons had been ordered as part of the armament for Fort Monroe, and in compliance with instructions from Washington, they were to be brought to the dock in Richmond by boat for reshipment. The matter of reshipment by boat was debated hotly in Richmond in the general assembly in late March, and the *Richmond Dispatch* said that "certainly the people of Chesterfield, Powhatan and Richmond will not permit this removal of arms to be effective at this juncture of affairs." Delegate Robertson offered a resolution on March 28 to prevent the transit of the guns through Richmond, and it was adopted, although some members called this step confiscation.[150]

A letter from the secretary of war to J.M. McCue of Virginia was published a few days later, denying that any order had been given to move the guns from Bellona Arsenal to Fort Monroe. On March 22, 1861, the *Enquirer* published the following letter from J.L. Archer, the superintendent of Bellona Foundry, to the ordnance office in Washington, showing that an order had been given:

Sir—You will please forward to Richmond the cannon at your foundry which have been inspected for the United States, with little delay as

Entrance of the Bellona area with cannon balls on a stone fence, 2018. *Courtesy of Charles Rose Real Estate.*

> *practicable; and as soon as they are shipped from that place, the amount due on the last inspection will be paid. The quartermaster's department has authorized Messrs. W.D. Colquitt & Co., ship brokers, to receive the guns and to attend to the re-shipment, and the delivery had better be made alongside the vessel that is to transport them to Fort Monroe Arsenal, for which the usual amount paid for hauling will be paid.*[151]

On January 1, 1863, Archer released both the arsenal and the foundry to the Confederacy, but he remained on the premises as superintendent. Local tradition would have one believe that Bellona Arsenal served in the 1860s as a vital military installation—that it was "Lee's secret munition source." Its neighbor, Bellona Foundry, was obviously useful, but no evidence has been found to substantiate the imagined importance of the arsenal in Confederate strategy.

With Virginia's secession and the advent of war in 1861, Archer rehabilitated Clarke's long-defunct munitions factory, and Bellona returned to its original incarnation as a weapons depot. Many Virginians who owned more slaves than they could profitably keep responded to the economic changes by leasing enslaved laborers to people and businesses who needed extra workers or domestic servants. The rapid expansion in cotton planting in the Deep South generated its own great demand for slaves, and Richmond emerged as the center of the massive interstate slave trade. It is likely that sale of slaves brought more money into Virginia than any other export.

It was uncertain what roles the war and President Abraham Lincoln would play in freeing the slaves. Lincoln was initially unsure and cautious about emancipating the slaves. On several occasions, Lincoln made it clear that his primary intention was to save the Union, regardless of the outcome as it related to slavery.[152] Virginia imported some 52,000 "slaves" between 1710 and 1769. While Virginians showed some preference for Africans from the Senegambian coast and hinterland, there was also a large number of Igbo men in the region because of the refusal of South Carolina planters to purchase them. Data also indicates that many of the slaves brought into Virginia came from the West Indies, where they had "already undergone an initial process of acculturation."[153]

Almost 500,000 Virginians, nearly one-third of the entire population of the state, lived in slavery in 1860. More enslaved people and more owners of slaves lived in Virginia than in any other state. A large majority of Virginia's enslaved people worked on farms and plantations, and most of them resided east of the Blue Ridge. The counties between the mountains and Chesapeake Bay, where tobacco cultivation retained prime economic importance, had the highest concentrations of enslaved people in the state. South of the Rappahannock River, about half of the region's population lived in slavery. In about a dozen counties, the enslaved population made up between 60 percent and 70 percent of the total population, and in two counties, Nottoway and Amelia, that number rose to between 70 and 75 percent. Of all the regional differences within the United States, the most important was where slavery was legal and where it was not legal. Likewise, within Virginia, the very uneven distribution of the enslaved population created distinct regional differences that influenced how people reacted to the secession crisis when it erupted at the end of 1860.[154]

The slaves constituted the lifeline of the Southern labor force. Not only were they found in all crafts, from the most specialized to the least specialized, but they were also in virtually every other important Southern industry. The skills acquired by these laborers increased their economic value and, often, their mobility. Owners frequently hired or leased the services of their slaves to other employers and plantation owners. Because slave artisans and mechanics were in great demand, they were frequently able to use their free time to perform extra work for money that they were allowed to keep for themselves; this money could eventually be used to purchase their freedom. It is safe to hypothesize that slave labor was utilized to the maximum extent in many of Clarke's building projects.[155]

A joint resolution regarding the movement of troops and arms within the limits of this commonwealth by the general government was adopted on April 1, 1861:

> *And whereas, it has come to the knowledge of this legislature that a large number of heavy guns manufactured at Bellona Foundry, near the capital of Virginia, under an order of the Ordnance Department at Washington, D.C., have been ordered to Fortress Monroe, where they can only be needed for the purpose of intimidation and menace to Virginia at present, and of actual hostilities in a certain contingency that may change her future relations to the federal government and the anti-slavery sentiment it represents:*
>
> *1. Be it resolved by the general assembly, that the governor of this commonwealth be authorized, and he is hereby directed, in case of the actual attempt of the federal authorities to transport said guns over the soil of Virginia, to seize and detain such guns for the use of this commonwealth; and to that end, to order out the public guard to arrest the contemplated removal of the guns beyond the reach and control of the government of this state.*
>
> *2. Resolved further, that the governor be, and he is hereby, authorized and required, out of the money appropriated for the purchase of arms at the present session of the general assembly, by an act passed on the 29th day of January, 1861, entitled and act appropriated $1,000,000 for the defense of the commonwealth, to pay to Dr. Junius L. Archer the amount due him, viz, $7,872.47, on his contract for the manufacture of said guns, and to the government at Washington the sum of $13,024, which said government has paid to said Archer on account of his said contract; and the governor shall require the superintendent of the armory at Richmond to take possession of said guns and deposit them therein for safe-keeping.[156]*

Much of the ordnance manufactured at Bellona saw service during the war with England, and for many years thereafter, the Clarke guns were used by the United States government, and those made by his successors were part of the early equipment of the Confederate fortifications guarding Richmond.

To test the guns after they were made, Major Clarke fired them down the James River while his workers were protected against a premature explosion or bursting muzzles by a high embankment on the shore. The Bellona guns were said to have been unsurpassed in quality by any manufactured in this country at the time. Major Clarke's foundry also turned out other iron products. In 1817, a cast-iron railing was advertised by him.[157]

There is nobody in Virginia who does not recollect the noise that was not made by but made about the guns of Dr. Junius Archer that were manufactured at Bellona in 1861.

> Archer projectiles are named after Dr. Junius L. Archer, owner of the Bellona Foundry. This projectile has two deep grooves on a tapered cone to help hold the lead sabot in firing. The majority of the fired Archer projectiles are found with the lead sabot missing. In the space between the lead ban and the projectile body was a lubricated hemp rope. During firing, this hemp rope was forced into the grooves of the cannon when the lead sabot expanded. The lubricant reduced friction and subsequent wear on the cannon. Similar specimens have been found in 3.3-inch caliber.[158]

The guns are more "interesting" because they came from Old Bellona, where good guns—guns that would hold together—were made at a time when they failed to be made anywhere else in the then United States. This was done, originally, under the supervision of the late Major Clarke, a man of decided mechanical genius, who constructed the armory, the most perfect model of a building for such a purpose in the world, as every mechanic knows. Major Clarke had no model to go by. He only consulted his own genius, and his work was a gem. He was afterward persecuted and pursued by bitter personal enemies until he threw up his office as superintendent of the armory and retired to his farm in Powhatan. On his own property, he established a foundry, and it was not long before he could have found employment for five such establishments as his.

> Contracts on a large scale were made in all parts of the county and among others with Major Clarke. When the guns came to be tested, the "burst up" was almost universal. But one lot stood the ordeal, and that was furnished by Major Clarke from Old Bellona, though it was not Old Bellona then. For several years, the experiments were repeated, and the Bellona guns were the only guns that could not be busted. Major Clarke's guns, at one time, did burst—a few of them at least—but Dr. Archer, as far as historians now recollect, never burst

but a single gun. The doctor had all the qualities of a good officer. He inherited the spirit of his race, and was, besides, an exceedingly popular man—a man of great kindness of disposition, excellent sense and a heart which never allowed him to overlook the wants of his soldiers.[159]

On January 1, 1863, both the arsenal and foundry were leased to the Confederacy. During the war, Bellona ranked second only to Richmond's famous Tredegar Ironworks as Virginia's leading producer of arms. The Manufacture of Arms was the third-largest producer of arms, operating adjacent to Tredegar. Demand for coal was great, and the price was high during the war, but the English companies did not seem interested in taking advantage of the situation by reopening their mines. Perhaps a hands-off policy existed because the coal would have been used to aid the Confederacy, and England refused to officially help the Confederate States. Other than the mines that were leased to the Midlothian Company, no record can be found of any English pits operating during the war, although several had been leased prior to that time.[160]

Dahlgren's Abortive Raid on Bellona

Exaggerated rumors that Bellona was Lee's "secret source" of munitions may have inspired Union Colonel Ulric Dahlgren's abortive raid on Richmond in 1864. In the spring of 1864, Colonel Ulric Dahlgren aimed to destroy Bellona as he attempted to invade Richmond. There was only one obstacle in his way: the James River. Dahlgren believed he could enter Richmond from the west and south. He gave some of his men orders to cross the James River from Goochland County at Dover Mills. From there, they would attack Bellona.

In order to arrive safely at Dover Mills, Colonel Dahlgren relied on the guidance of a runaway slave named Martin Robinson. Robinson agreed to guide the cavalry to a ford where some of them could cross the river and then blaze a destructive path along the south side of the route to Richmond. The agreement made clear that Robinson would be executed if he was found guilty of misleading the men. The cavalry rode in the rain for two nights to Dover Mills. When they arrived, they were very surprised to find that there was not a ford; the river was deep and swift, and they could not cross. Lieutenant Bartley of the United States Signal Corps witnessed the event and wondered why Robinson would mislead Dahlgren when his own life was on the line. Bartley described the result of the perceived treachery: "The

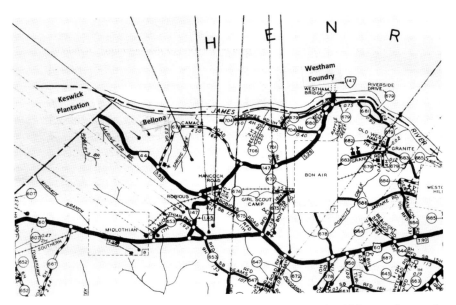

1936 map of Camack Road, now Old Gun Road, and the connecting highways. *Courtesy of Chesterfield County Library.*

Southern Church Hill view of the river, overlooking Libby Hill, before the war. *Photograph courtesy of M. Robinson.*

colonel then told him he would have to carry out his part of the contract, to which the guide assented, and admitted that was the agreement and made no objection of his execution. He went along to the tree without any force and submitted to his fate without a murmur." Dahlgren left Robinson's body hanging in the tree and pushed on to Richmond without crossing the river to the Bellona side. The colonel was later killed by a Confederate ambush. After the war, local witnesses stated that winter rains had swollen the James River, inundating the ford that is passable most of the year. Bellona was spared by a flood. Martin Robinson was betrayed by it.[161]

The Bellona Arsenal (q.v.) was the military post garrisoned by a battery of U.S. artillery. It was located fourteen miles north of Richmond, adjacent to Bellona Foundry (q.v.), and it served as a facility for repair and fabrication of small arms and other munitions. It presumably also received the stored cannon produced for the government at the nearby foundry. It was also referred to as the Bellona Foundry Arsenal (B.F.A.) for purpose of putting these initials on the weapons it produced. The initials B.A. were found stamped on a few of the artillery pieces produced.

The Chesterfield Heavy Artillery and the Southside Heavy Artillery, recruited respectively by Captains Drewry and Jones, manned the huge guns, most of which had been manufactured at Bellona Foundry. Many of the gunners came directly from Chesterfield farms and were beyond the conscription (draft) age.[162]

Burials in the Trabue Cemetery at Bellona Arsenal
1889–1929

Date of Death	Family members
1832	Sarah Frances Trabue Young, 1785–1832, daughter of William Trabue, who died April 11, 1827
October 15, 1848	John Stanford
March 17, 1882	Whitfield Turnley
May 26, 1882	Charles W. Turnley
July 30, 1889	Luther Watts Turnley
July 19, 1889	Luther Joseph Turnley
1903	Sarah Frances Stanford Young, born 1820
April 16, 1923	John McBride
1929	David S. Young, born October 26, 1851
1929	Jefferson D. Young, born October 26, 1851

Other burials with unknown complete names and dates:

Two boys, John Young, Grandma Young, Reverend Joseph Peace Young (husband of Sarah Young), Uncle Jeff, Joseph T. Young (born February 19, 1856), Donald S. Young, Miss Molly Young, Mary Sarah Adams (daughter of Sarah Frances), Jacob Trabue, Reverend Joseph P. Young and the sister-in-law of John McBride.

Frightened Chesterfield Courthouse residents watched from the sidelines as observers and couriers reported to headquarters in Richmond that the enemy, with almost three thousand men and six howitzers, passed through Chesterfield Courthouse on May 12, 1864, at about 1:00 p.m.

KAUTZ'S ABORTIVE RAID ON BELLONA

Observers also reported that they believed rumors that the raiders were headed for the Richmond and Danville Railroad and Bellona Arsenal and Foundry on the James River, about six miles above Richmond. The observers further predicted that the enemy would attempt to reach Richmond from the arsenal via the James River Road.[163] Before leaving the smoking ruins at Coalfield Station, Captain Kautz and his officers discussed an attack but then decided against a move on nearby Bellona Arsenal and Foundry, believing it was too heavily guarded.[164]

In 1864, the Civil War had been dragging on for three years. Stepped-up shipments of local coal fueled the furnaces at nearby Bellona Foundry and at the Tredegar Iron Works in Richmond.[165] The Confederate Congress subsequently adopted a joint resolution to reimburse Dr. Archer in the sum of $8,000 for what he had not collected from the United States for the undeliverable guns. The Confederate War Department, in the meantime, gave Dr. Archer contracts for ordnance: one calling for the delivery of fifty twenty-four-, forty-two- and sixty-eight-pounders. For these guns, carriages were needed, and some were made for them in Richmond and Danville's Manchester shops. When the war got under way, the Bellona plant received additional orders.[166]

Around 8:00 a.m., when Richmond fell, the fire reached the Richmond Arsenal and the heavy ammunition, which included one hundred thousand shells stockpiled in the yard. The Gorgas family had left their living quarters at the armory the previous evening. The armory and all its ammunition went

Original tops that were saved after the penitentiary buildings were destroyed in the late 1860s. *Courtesy of Tredegar Iron Works Inc., Richmond, Virginia.*

up in an explosion that lasted for four hours. When the fire burned itself out, the armory complex was demolished, only its smoking ruins remained.

Despite the considerable number of spies and friends the Union had in Richmond and the surrounding area, it is said that the North did not know until after the war that General Lee's men never lacked the ammunition, right up until the last days at Appomattox.[167]

At the end of the war, the federal government claimed the property.[168]

CHANGE OF OWNERSHIP

BELLONA'S FOUNDRY AND ARSENAL AREA

1607	First English settlers in the area
1687	Antoine Pierre Trabue
1724	William Trabue
1750	Major John Clarke
1772	Major Clarke and William Wirt
1801	W. Trabue to Kitty Bryers, 40.5 acres
1807	W. Trabue to Philip Turbin, 176 acres
	Turbin to Phillis Logan, 18.75 acres
1810	Clarke's Foundry built
1815	Jacob and John Trabue to U.S. government, 27.5 acres
1817	Bellona Arsenal built by government
1837	Leased to Thomas M. Randolph
1844	Farm inherited by Dr. Junius L. Archer
	Archer obtained 178 acres from the estate of Joseph P. Young
1856	Arsenal property inherited by Dr. Archer
1861	Virginia governor, Civil War
	Temporarily rented by J.R. Anderson of Tredegar Iron Works
	Mourning Logan bought 18.5 acres
1863	Leased to the Confederacy
1865	Bellona was never destroyed by the Union
	Virginia Manufactory of Arms destroyed by the Union

KESWICK PLANTATION AREA

1687	Antoine Trabue
1724	William Trabue
1732	Charles Clarke, Manor House
1740s	Colonel James Clarke
1750	Major John Clarke, Keswick
c.1800	John Clarke's house built
1844	Death of John Clarke
1844	Clarke's two daughters and two grandchildren assume ownership

GAMBLE'S HILL

1750	Gamble's Hill's construction began
1776	Westham built
1781	Westham destroyed
1785	Kanawha Canal's construction began
1797	Penitentiary built
1802	Manufactory built
1808	Armory scandal
1837	Tredegar built
1845	Manufactory idled
1865	Manufactory destroyed

VIRGINIA MANUFACTORY OF ARMS

1798	Clarke drew plans to build
1799	Construction began
1802	Existed next to Tredegar Iron Works
1809	Large cannon foundry operation
1820	Grew out of arms quota
1821	Building out of arms operation
1861	Name changed during Civil War to Richmond Armory and Richmond Arsenal
1863	Lab department exploded, killing forty-five
1865	Building was destroyed by the Union
1865	Manufactory and Amory destroyed

CONCLUSION

Now, the secrets of Early Richmond in the sixteenth and seventeenth centuries are out for everyone to appreciate and learn. There were many hidden areas in Richmond and Chesterfield that were discovered during this exciting period. For instance, the hidden history of the first Huguenot settlers and the arsenals and armories operating in Richmond and Bellona. By reading this book, you have lived through how Richmonders began with the development of the initial Seven Hills, which are somewhat hidden today. This book tells a unique story of the people and the events they shared during this time. Readers also learned how one would have produced silk during this period. And don't forget, this story also took you through the pains that Richmond suffered during the Civil War.

CHRONOLOGICAL HISTORY

1607	First English settlers set foot in northern Chesterfield County.
1687	Antoine Pierre Trabue (1667–1724), a French Huguenot who fled Montauban, France, in 1687 and migrated to Virginia, owned property in both Powhatan and Midlothian.
1600s	First Europeans saw a Native American village in Richmond that was referred to as Powhatantown.
	Slavery was legalized in Virginia; however, there were only three hundred enslaved Africans in the Virginia Colony in 1649.
1700s	A grant of ten thousand acres was given in the early 1700s by British King William III to several French Huguenot refugees for settlement above the James River on the Piedmont frontier.
	The settlement was known as Manakintown.
	The Manor House was the first building on the Keswick property. It was constructed by Charles Clarke.
	Slaves opened their own churches against the law that stated it was illegal to have a black minister.

1702	Coal was discovered in Midlothian area, but forty-eight years passed before it was commercially produced.
1716	Jacob Amonet was granted two patents for 274 acres, and he built a residence that he called Bellona Arsenal.
1724	Antoine died, and his sons inherited his properties; 26.5 acres were conveyed to the government by Antoine, Polly Trabue and Mary Reddy.
	William Trabue owned the sites and built an arsenal in Powhatan.
1737	Richmond Hill was laid out as a city by Colonel William Mayo.
1749	Chesterfield was officially established and named for Philip Dormer Stanhope, the fourth earl of Chesterfield.
1750	The Huguenots deserted Manakintown.
	Manor House was situated on part of a 1,500-acre land grant made to Charles Clarke in the early 1700s.
1766	John Clarke was born at Keswick.
1776–1781	Westham Foundry existed across and beside the river.
1700s	Point of Fork Arsenal, located in Columbia, Virginia, was destroyed in 1781, rebuilt and abandoned for Virginia Manufactory of Arms in 1801.
1777	Powhatan County was created by the Virginia General Assembly.
1779	Richmond was declared the capital of Virginia.
1780	Virginia's capital was officially moved from Williamsburg to Richmond.
1782	Half of every one thousand Richmond residents were slaves.
1790	The first official U.S. census was recorded, and Richmond County was credited with 14,514 residents.
1791	John Clarke married Elizabeth Moseley of Powhatan.
Late 1700s	Before the end of the eighteenth century, John Clarke was a well-known Powhatan millwright.

1794	Major John Clarke (1766–1844) built the state armory at Gamble's Hill and Latrobe's State Penitentiary.
1797	The Virginia General Assembly chose Clarke to design, build and operate the Virginia Manufactory of Arms.
	The penitentiary's cornerstone was laid with Henry Latrobe's name as architect.
1798	The Virginia General Assembly established the Virginia Manufactory of Arms.
	Clarke was appointed as the superintendent of the state armory in 1798.
Early 1800s	John Clarke's house was built at Keswick on the Powhatan County line.
	Clarke built Keswick next to Bellona.
1801	The purchase of 40.5 acres by Kitty Bryers from William Trabue was included in the 176 acres.
	A small rectangular window, suggested by John Clarke, was created in the storage area over the portico of the state capitol (see added windows in 1862).
1802	Major Clarke was connected with the Virginia State Arsenal in Richmond.
1804	A turnpike toward Richmond was opened in Midlothian.
1806	John Clarke's wife died.
1807	The sale of 176 acres from Kitty Bryers to Phillip Turpin took place.
	Turpin, in turn, sold 18.75 acres to Phillis Logan, a woman of color.
1808	Clarke was reelected as the superintendent of the Virginia Manufactory of Arms.
1809	Clarke of Powhatan County was forced out of office.
1810	Clarke and William Wirt (1772–1834) established an iron foundry near Keswick.
	Bellona Foundry was located one-quarter mile from Bellona Arsenal; it is also called Bellona Foundry Arsenal.

1812	The projected war arsenal was named Bellona, after the goddess of war.
	The War of 1812 began in Virginia.
1813	Keswick produced the cannons and shot used in the War of 1812.
Early 1814	John Clarke, whose home was the plantation of Keswick, convinced the war department to build an arsenal near his foundry
1814	Bellona Foundry's workshop was built, first on one hundred acres on the James River, near Spring Creek.
1815	Clarke and Wirt negotiated to cast three hundred tons of army cannons.
	Clarke's foundry built "quality" swords, rifles, muskets and projectiles.
	The foundry operated, apparently steadily, from 1815 to 1869.
July 24, 1815	Lundsford Tayloe Lomax, the son of Major M.P. Lomax of the U.S. Army, died at Bellona Arsenal.
September 15, 1815	William Trabue conveyed 27.5 acres to the government through Jacob and John James Trabue, the sons of Antoine, to build the arsenal.
1815–1817	The construction of the arsenal proper started, and it was garrisoned by ordinance troops.
1816	Robert Leckie (Lecky), the supervisor and master mason, started the arsenal's construction.
	Clarke submitted the plans for landscaping the capitol grounds, but they were rejected.
Late 1816	The powder magazine's construction began.
1816–1817	Construction of Bellona Arsenal and Power Mill was completed
1816–1821	The Bellona post was garrisoned by ordnance troops.
1816–1830s	Numerous slaves worked within the arsenal.
1816–1832	The U.S. Government (War Department) owned Bellona.

1816	A graveyard for free people of color and slaves was established at Shockoe Hill.
1817	A twelve-acre foundry partnership agreement was recorded between Clarke and Wirt.
	The arsenal received and stored cannons from the foundry.
	Stone walls enclosed eight arsenal buildings surrounding the quadrangle.
	Major Clarke also turned out cast-iron railings and cookpots at Bellona.
July 1817	James Clarke sold a lot each to two men of color.
October 1817	Buildings of brick and stone were erected by the government in Bellona.
August 1818	Philip and Martha Turpin set an enslaved family of ten, with seven adults and three children, free.
1820s	A grove of trees was planted to ward off the harmful "miasmas" that rose from the river and infected the air.
1821–1831	A company of artillery was stationed at the Richmond Arsenal.
1821	The production of arms at the manufactory ceased.
1823	The state library was founded in Richmond.
April 11, 1827	William Trabue was buried on the Bellona property.
1827–1929	Seven unmarked graves, with one marked stone (Trabue), were established.
Mar 3, 1819, and April 28, 1828	The government tried to abolish Bellona Arsenal twice.
1828	The B&O Railroad Company chartered the first railway in Virginia.
1830	A simple window appeared in the state capitol's dome, as suggested by Clarke.
1830s	A mysterious round building was built at Keswick.

1831	The Virginia General Assembly was ready to abolish the Richmond slave trade prior to the Nat Turner Rebellion.
1832	The arms reparation center was relocated to Fort Monroe.
	Bellona was shutting down operations.
	Ordnance Sergeant Moses McArthur was put in charge as military caretaker.
	Sarah Frances Trabue Young was buried at Bellona.
1833	The arsenal area was abandoned as a military reservation.
1834	Nine more guns blew up when test fired by ordnance inspectors.
1835	Bosher Dam was built across the James River, and the construction of the Kanawha Canal continued.
1836	A statement concerning the arsenals and armories of the United States, under the resolution of the Senate, was released.
	Midlothian Coal Mining Company was organized.
	Richmond, Fredericksburg & Potomac Railroad opened Richmond to Hazel Run.
1837	Bellona Arsenal was declared surplus property by the War Department.
	Tredegar Iron Works was opened for business.
1837–1840	A silkworm farm was developed at Bellona.
	The silkworm farm was leased to Thomas Mann Randolph.
1838	The great American silk-raising boom started.
1840–1842	Randolph's partner, Thomas S. Pleasants Jr., and Henry Clarke operated the silk farm.
1842	The experiment to raise silk failed.
May 1844	Major John Clarke died and was buried at Keswick Plantation.

1844–1853	The farm was inherited by Dr. Junius L. Archer, the grandson of Clarke.
	Archer obtained 178 acres from the estate of Joseph P. Young.
1848	John Stanford was buried on the Bellona property.
October 15, 1848	John Stanford, the husband of Sarah Frances Trabue, was buried.
1853	Jefferson Davis sold some land to Phillip St. George Cocke.
1856	Archer purchased the entire arsenal property for $2,650 from General Philip St. George Cocke.
1858	John Clarke's lunette window appears in the south pediment of the capitol.
1859	The ordnance department refused cannons not cast by the Rodman method.
Until 1860	Bellona Foundry turned out cannons, shot, swords and firearms.
1860	The manufactory was rebuilt and retooled after the raid in Harpers Ferry.
Early 1861	Joseph R. Anderson of Tredegar briefly rented Bellona Foundry.
	The Confederate capital was moved to Richmond on May 8, 1861.
1861	Bellona was sold and taken over by the Virginia governor.
	Bellona Arsenal was back in operation during the Civil War.
	Mourning Logan purchased 18.5 acres again.
	Archer's foundry made ordnance for the Confederacy.
	Bellona property was claimed by the government from General Cocke and Dr. Archer.
	The Virginia Manufactory of Arms was revived at the beginning of the Civil War.
1862	Three additional windows were added to the state capitol's storage area over the portico (see first window in 1801).

May 15, 1862	The first major action of the Civil War in Chesterfield County took place.
1862	Two quarter circle windows were added to the state capitol.
January 1863	Archer leased Bellona Arsenal and Foundry to the Confederate government.
February 1863	A federal raider passed by the foundry.
April 1863	A fire damaged the Bellona Foundry.
1863	The Emancipation Proclamation technically freed all Richmond "contrabands" in the spring of 1865.
1864	Bellona rumors led the Union raid on Richmond.
	Rumors that Bellona was Lee's "secret source" of munitions inspired Union colonel Dahlgren's abortive raid on Richmond.
1865	The Civil War closed as Lee retreated and surrendered at Appomattox.
	The Virginia Manufactory of Arms was gutted by fire during the evacuation of Richmond.

NOTES

Epigraph

1. The original 1805 letter is in the John Clarke Letter Book, Special Collections, Library of Virginia.

Chapter 1

2. "Monacan Indian Nations," www.monacannation.net.
3. The Millau Viaduct spans the valley of the River Tarn near Millau and is now one of the area's most popular attractions.
4. Yates, *Trabue Family*.
5. "Powhatan County, Virginia," www.wikipedia.com.
6. The original is in the Edwin Markham Archives, Horrmann Library, Wagner College, Staten Island, NY.
7. Huguenot Society of Founders of Manakin in the Colony of Virginia, www.huguenotmanakin.org; Huguenots Emigrants of the James River, VCU Library Reports; Document at the Virginia Historical Society, Antoine Trabue and "The Escape of Anthony Trabue" by Daniel Trabue, 4–5.
8. This Virginia State Settlement Marker (0-28) and description was set up by the Department for Historic Resources in 2000 on Midlothian Turnpike in Midlothian, Virginia.

Chapter 2

9. Lutz, *Chesterfield*. Chesterfield's part of the parish (county) was either dormant or became extinct in 1850, when Powhatan was given a slice of the county's area in straightening the boundary line.

10. Ibid. The only dry segment of the boundary was the line between Chesterfield and the then-Goochland County, which, since 1777, has been the eastern border of the present Powhatan County.

11. Keswick, *Homes and Gardens*, 187–89.

12. Moseley, *Huguenot Houses*, 11.

13. Women's Committee of Richmond, *Historic Keswick*.

14. Moseley, *Two Huguenot Houses*.

15. United States Department of the Interior, National Park Service, National Register of Historic Places Inventory, Prepared by Junius R. Fishburne Jr., executive director, November 19, 1974. The parapeted gables, jack arches, Flemish-bond façade and traditional plan and stairs of the brick building argue for its being built slightly earlier than the main house and its other outbuildings.

16. Singletary, *Spirits Know*, 4.

17. United States Department of the Interior, National Park Service, National Register of Historic Places Inventory, prepared by Junius R. Fishburne Jr., executive director, November 19, 1974.

18. *Powhatan County Archives, Virginia Historic Architectural Survey*, November 25, 1991, Traceries, 1606 Twentieth Street, N.W., Washington, D.C. 20001, Keswick, VDHR 072-0045-001.

19. Holloway, *Slave Rebellion*. The building's design is of Kongo and Central African origin; the circular geometric design is typical of structures built by Africans from that region. There are several examples of this design found in the book *Drums and Shadows*. West African style is generally rectangular in design. Farris Thompson may have mentioned this design in *Flash of the Spirit*. All the early reports of African huts in the Kongo confirm this.

20. Ross, "Why Our Ancestors Built Round Houses?" www.inhabitat.com.

21. Reginald Nalugale, PhD, *Development, Poverty and Faith* (Oxford, UK: Oxford Center for Mission Studies, 2007); Elwyn Jenkins, *Why are Traditional African Huts Round?*

22. National Register, United States, 1.

23. Singletary, *Spirits Know*, 5.

24. Barnett, "Richmond Architect," 49.

25. Lutz, *Chesterfield*, 70.

Chapter 3

26. Woodlief, *River Times.*
27. *American-Made Light Artillery in the Revolution*, August 14, 2014, administered by the Jamestown-Yorktown Foundation, an agency of the Commonwealth of Virginia, accredited by the American Alliance of Museums, Jamestown-Yorktown Foundation, P.O. Box 1607, Williamsburg, Virginia 23187-1607.
28. State Records Collection, Public Foundry at Westham Accounts, 1781–1792, Library of Virginia, Auditor of Public Accounts (Record Group 48).
29. Marie Tyler-McGraw, *At the Falls: Richmond, Virginia and Its People* (Chapel Hill, NC: University of North Carolina Press, 1994.)
30. Point of Fork Arsenal was established in the eighteenth century and located near Columbia, Fluvanna County. It was raided and destroyed in 1781; it was rebuilt and remained in service until 1801. It was abandoned in 1801 in favor of a more centralized arsenal in Richmond, the Virginia Manufactory of Arms.
31. Minutes from the general assembly show that the canal on Southside Street was approved by the general assembly in 1817 and was nearly completed by 1833.
32. Major John Clarke was an expert in canal engineering, as demonstrated by his letter to Thomas M. Randolph, the governor of Virginia, which he wrote from Keswick in Powhatan, on February 9, 1820. James River and Kanawha Company (Richmond, VA), records, 1835–1881, Accession 36027, business records collection, Library of Virginia.
33. Benedict Arnold, "Arnold's Expedition to Richmond, Virginia, 1781," *William and Mary Quarterly*, 2nd series, 12 (July 1932): 189.
34. William Feltman, Journal, 8; Hendricks, *Backcountry Towns*, 43.
35. Hendricks, *Backcountry Towns.*
36. Kerby, *Midlothian*, 23.
37. *Messenger*, January 2002.
38. Lutz, "Pesky Redcoats Again," 161.
39. Property of the Wanganui District Council Information and Images, courtesy of Geoff Lawson, compiled by John Osborne; Cannons from the ship *Lady Dennison*, which ran aground in the mouth of the Wanganui River in 1865. Courtesy of the Royal New Zealand Artillery Association Inc.
40. *Bellona Foundry*, 1.
41. Ibid., 38.

42. Department of Conservation and Historic Recourses, Bellona Arsenal Highway Marker, 1927, located on Midlothian Turnpike, Midlothian, Virginia.

43. One of the best legal talents in the state.

44. *Bellona Foundry*, 7.

45. James Clarke of Powhatan, an agent on behalf of the proprietors of the town of Swansborough, sold a man of color to Edward B. Edwards for money and a lot on the south side of Turnpike Road containing one acre along with a slip of land adjacent which makes it lot no. 1.

46. *Bellona Foundry*, 7.

47. Ibid., 26.

48. Ibid., 2.

49. Dennis P. Farmer, "Bellona, Cast for War," *Messenger*, January 2002.

50. Hunter, "Sound of the Guns."

51. Property of the Wanganui District.

52. *Bellona Foundry*, 5.

53. National Register of Historic Places, Bellona Arsenal, December 18, 1970.

54. Lutz, "Pesky Redcoats Again," 162.

55. Weaver, *Midlothian*, 43.

56. Wilkes, *Virginia Division*; Department of Mines, Minerals and Energy and Division of Mineral Resources, Charlottesville, VA, 44–45.

57. Wilkes, *Virginia Division*, 35.

58. Lutz, *Chesterfield*, 228–29. During the Richmond Secession Convention of April 1981, a public controversy raged over the disposition of fifty Columbiads manufactured for the U.S. War Department at Bellona Foundry. In late March, the *Richmond Dispatch* stated, "Certainly the people of Chesterfield, Powhatan and Richmond will not permit this removal of arms to be effective at this juncture of affairs." The shipment of the cannons was delayed by various pretexts until Virginia's secession solved the problem in favor of their detention. Several of the guns later saw use at Drewrys Bluff.

59. Civil War Artillery, "Federal and Confederate Manufacturers," www.civilwarartillery.com.

60. Chesterfield County Historic Sites and Structures, Bellona Arsenal, Military Sites and Structures, 389.

61. Barnett, "Richmond Architect," 44.

62. Lutz, *Chesterfield*, 162.

63. *Bellona Foundry*, 35.

64. Lee, *Lee's City*.
65. *Bellona Foundry*, 35.
66. Hunter, "Sound of the Guns."
67. Chesterfield County Historic Sites and Structures, Bellona Foundry (ruins), 412.
68. The distinguishing structures that differentiate a cannon foundry from a nonmilitary foundry appear to be the boring mill and the testing areas.
69. *Bellona Foundry*, 9–10.
70. Ibid., 22.
71. Ibid., 47.
72. Ibid., 22.
73. Ibid., 23.

Chapter 4

74. Mrs. Maude Adkins Joyner, *Story of Historic Sites and People of Chesterfield County, Virginia*, Chesterfield, VA: Chesterfield Main Library, 1950.
75. Weaver, *Midlothian*, 22.
76. Josiah Gorgas, Cullum Register Book.
77. Ibid.
78. Fisher, *Archaeological Investigation*, 6, 7, 13.
79. Cromwell, *Manufactory of Arms*.
80. John Clarke, "Purchase Tobacco Warehouse and Build a Wall," letter, 1802.
81. Barnett, "Richmond Architect," 36.
82. Couture, *Powhatan*, 112.
83. Barnett, "Richmond Architect," 38.
84. Mark K. Greenough, "The Tour Supervisor and Historian at the Virginia State Capitol," www.lva.virginia.gov.
85. Barnett, "Richmond Architect," 37.
86. Laura Kamoie, Neabsco and Occoquan (Prince William, VA: L.C. Kamoie, 1998), 9.
87. Barnett, "Richmond Architect," 20.
88. "A Guide to the Virginia Manufactory of Arms Records, 1798–1886," Library of Virginia; On this Day, "23 January 1798: Virginia Manufactory of Arms," Virginia Historical Society, www.virginiahistory.org; Watkins Norvell, *Richmond, Virginia: Colonial, Revolutionary, Confederate and the Present* (Richmond, VA: E.B. Brown), 32.

89. Couture, "Powhatan Worthies," 111.
90. Library of Virginia Archives.
91. Barnett, "Richmond Architect," 24.
92. Ibid., 10.
93. Poteet, "Armory Scandal."
94. Lutz, "Pesky Redcoats Again," 168.
95. "Bellona Arsenal," *Homes*, 1931, 193–94.
96. Ibid., 194.
97. Photograph owned by *Times-Dispatch* Archives, Richmond, VA, early 1940s.
98. Woodson, "Hive of History."
99. Lutz, "Pesky Redcoats Again," 169.
100. Bruce, *Iron Manufacture.*
101. *Bellona Foundry*, 7.
102. Ibid., 95. Randolph was one of the Manchesters trustees in late 1700s.
103. Gaines, "Guns, Silkworms, and Pigs," 32–37.

Chapter 5

104. According to a 1937 ordinance by the City of Richmond, these were the seven official hills in the city of Richmond, with Gambles Hill including the Virginia Manufactory of Arms.
105. The name used especially in Britain and Ireland (and throughout the world among Anglicans and Methodists) for the Christian festival of Pentecost, the seventh Sunday after Easter, which commemorates the descent of the Holy Spirit upon Christ's disciples.
106. Lee, *Lee's City.*
107. Palmer, *Gamble's Hill.*
108. Lee, *Lee's City.*
109. The author had the privilege of establishing a chapter of the Richmond Jaycees in the late 1970s with a hand-picked group of prisoners at the Richmond penitentiary. The chapter was a success, but the prison visits left me with a greater appreciation of the inmates, guards and just being locked up in the facility itself.
110. The Library of Virginia. Benjamin Henry Latrobe (1794–1820), *Department of Corrections Collection*, Record Group 42, Richmond, Virginia.
111. T. Tyler Potterfield, "James River and Kanawha Canal: Timeline and Visual Documentation," n.p., August 2013.
112. Kollatz, "Mystery Basin," 2.

113. Ibid.

114. Ibid.

115. Calvin Schermerhorn, *Money over Mastery Family over Freedom: Slavery in the Antebellum Upper South* (Baltimore, MD: John Hopkins University, 2011).

116. Scott, *Old Richmond.*

117. Ibid., 261.

118. Ibid., 267.

119. Chesterfield County Deed Book 22, 1817–1819, LVA Reel no. 9, 336–39, "Philip Turpin and Martha Turpin of Chesterfield, in consideration of faithful industrious, honest and meritorious services rendered us by the following negroes, to wit, Billy, Daniel, Simon, Robert and Nanny as also David and his wife Lizzy with their children Frances, William and Alex as well as for divers other good causes and considerations do emancipate and set free....And it is our natural wish that they may be permitted to remain in the state of Virginia, should they prefer doing so, unmolested and uninjured, it being our determination that they should henceforth forever hereafter be discharged from bondage."

120. Ibid., 262.

121. Harry Kollatz Jr., "Neighborhood North of Leigh Street Not Forgotten," *Richmond Magazine*, November 1998.

122. Scott, *Old Richmond*, 279.

123. Library of Virginia, www.virginiamemory.com.

124. Civil War Richmond, www.civilwarrichmond.com.

125. Richmond, *Whig*, September 10, 1861.

126. Kimball, *American City, Southern Place*, 142–43.

127. Ibid.

128. Ibid., 74.

129. Kimball. "James Bahen," *in Dictionary of Virginia Biography: Vol. 1, Aaroe-Blanchfield*, ed. John T. Kneebone et al. (Richmond: Library of Virginia, 1998), 282–83

130. Ibid., 259–64, 282–83.

131. Zehmer, *Church Hill*, 13.

132. On the map, RF&P Railroad had tracks on Broad Street, down to Seventh Street, where it had a railroad depot. Between 1861 and 1865, RF&P had 133 black employees. Indeed, the black labor force of the RF&P Railroad Company played no small part in the vital war service of the seventy-five-mile-long line.

133. Ibid., 12.

134. The name Richmond Hill was often used in place of Church Hill; this name is found in newspapers as early as 1806 and as late as 1852.

Chapter 6

135. Lutz, *Chesterfield*, 140. Randolph purchased 1,350 acres from Salle in 1777 and built Salisbury, which was adjacent to Bellona. Salisbury, which was built as a hunting lodge during the eighteenth century by the Randolph family, stood directly across the James River from the Randolph plantation, Tuckahoe. As the governor of Virginia in 1784, Patrick Henry rented the 1,500-acre farm from Thomas Mann Randolph. Later, while Salisbury still served as the home of Governor Henry, Mr. Randolph sold the estate to Dr. Philip Turpin, a graduate of the University of Edinburgh. During the Revolutionary War, Dr. Turpin, while en route from Scotland to Virginia, was captured by the British. His possessions, including Salisbury, were confiscated.

136. Gaines, *Thomas Mann Randolph*.

137. Lutz, *Chesterfield*. Thomas Mann Randolph, who married one of Colonel Cary's daughters, purchased 1,350 acres from Abraham Salle in 1777 and built the original Salisbury. It was probably used as a hunting lodge, and it was leased by Randolph to Patrick Henry as his gubernatorial home.

138. Barnett, "Richmond Architect," 40.

139. Lutz, "Golden Dreams," 197–98.

Chapter 7

140. R.E. Johnson, *Tredegar Iron Works of Richmond, Virginia*, (n.p.:n.d) 56.

141. Knopp, *Richmond Arsenal*.

142. The addition of small amounts of water to the mixture can also be used to extend the burning time.

143. Mallet, "Ordnance."

144. *The Photographic History of the Civil War*, Volume III, Forts and Artillery, The Ordnance of the Confederacy.

145. Bellona Foundry 44 CF 118, 27, archaeological report.

146. Dew, *Ironmaker*, 78, 87.

147. U.S. Department of Agriculture, Cultural History of George Washington Jefferson National Forest, Forest Supervisor's Office, Roanoke, VA.

148. Calisch, "Bellona."

149. "Bellona Foundry," 32.

150. Lutz, *Chesterfield*, 118.

151. "The Bellona Arsenal Guns," *Daily Dispatch*, April 3, 1861.

152. Library of Virginia, Union or Secession 1961.

153. Singletary, *Spirits Know*, 1.

154. Virginia Memory, "Union or Secession-Virginia Decide," Library of Virginia, www.lva.virginia.gov; *An 1861 map showing the distribution of Virginia's "slave" population*, E. Hergesheimer, C.B. Graham, lithographer; *Map of Virginia Showing the Distribution of its Slave Population from the Census of 1860*, (Washington, D.C.: Henry S. Graham, 1861), Library of Virginia.

155. Singletary, *Spirits Know*, 4.

156. "The War of the Rebellion," a compilation of the official records of the Union and Confederate armies, published under the direction of the Honorable Elihu Root, secretary of war, by Brigadier General Fred C. Ainsworth, chief of the Record and Pension Office, War Department, and Mr. Joseph W. Kinkley, series 4, vol. 1 (Washington, D.C.: Government Printing Office, 1900).

157. Lutz, "Pesky Redcoats Again," 162.

158. Old Glory Prints, www.oldgloryprints.com.

159. "'The Guns'—Junius Archer—the late Major John Clarke," *Daily Dispatch*, April 27, 1861; Cowardin and Hammersley, *Richmond Dispatch*.

160. Burtchett, "Village of Midlothian," 51.

161. Lorne Field, "When the James was a Cauldron of Conflict," *Richmond Newspaper*, February 18, 2014. Lorne Field is the environmental outreach coordinator for the Chesterfield County Department of Environmental Engineering.

162. Lutz, *Chesterfield*, 236.

163. Weaver, *Midlothian*, 58.

164. Captain August Valentine Kautz, a German American soldier in the Union Army and cavalry officer during the American Civil War with the Sixth U.S. Cavalry; Weaver, *Midlothian*, 60–61.

165. Weaver, *Midlothian*, 55.

166. Lutz, "Gathering War Clouds," 229.

167. Calisch, "Bellona," 7.

168. Chesterfield County Historic Sites and Structures, 389.

Bibliography

Appich, J.R. "Historic Keswick: Classic Plantation Elegance 1993." *Richmond Family Magazine*, 1993.

Archives of the Library of Virginia. *Virginia Memory & Virginia Cavalcade*. Richmond: Library of Virginia, 1607–1865.

Barnett, Elizabeth Johnson. "John Clarke (1766–1844) Richmond Architect and Industrialist." Thesis, Virginia Commonwealth Universary, 2001.

Bellona-Rodin Museum.

Bradbury, Eugene. *Historic American Buildings Survey*. Richmond, VA: Fb&C Limited, 1937.

Browning, Lyle. "Bellona Foundry." *Messenger*, 1992.

Bruce, Kathleen. *Virginia Iron Manufacture in the Slave Era*. New York: Century Co., 1931.

Bugg, James L., Jr. "The French Huguenot Frontier Settlement of Manakin Towns." *Virginia Magazine of History and Biography*, October 1953.

Burtchett. "A History of the Village of Midlothian, Virginia." Thesis, University of Richmond, 1983.

Calisch, A. Woolner. "Bellona, the Arms Depot of the Confederacy." Chesterfield Historical Society of Virginia, 1937.

Chesterfield County Deed Book. Virginia Slaves Freed After 1782, 1817–1819. LVA reel no. 9.

Chesterfield County Public Libraries. www.library.chesterfield.gov.

Christian, Francis Auther. "Homes and Gardens in Old Virginia." *California Magazine*, 1931.

Couture, Richard T. *Powhatan, A Bicentennial History*. Powhatan County, VA: Dietz Press, 1980.

Cromwell, Giles. *The Manufactory of Arms*. Charlottesville: University Press of Virginia, 1975.

Daily Dispatch. "The Chesterfield Historical Society." April 27, 1861.

Department of Conservation and Historic Resources. www.dhr.virginia.gov.

Dew, Charles B. *Ironmaker to the Confederacy*. New Haven, CT: Yale Universary Press, 1999.

Farley, James J. *Making Arms in the Machine Age: 1816–1870*. University Park, PA: University Press, 1994.

Fisher, H. Garrison. *The Archaeological Investigations of the Virginia Manufactory of Arms*. Richmond, VA: Univerity of Richmond, 1988.

Gaines, William Harris, Jr. "Guns, Silkworms, and Pigs." *Virginia Cavalcade*, 1953.

———. *Thomas Mann Randolph-Jefferson's Son-in-Law*. Baton Rouge: Louisiana State University Press, 1966.

Gorman, Mike. "Civil War Richmond Digital Library." www.mdgorman.com.

Haskett, James J. "An Investigation of the History of the Virginia Manufactory of Arms."

Hendricks, Christopher. *The Backcountry Towns of Colonial Virginia*. Knoxville: University of Tennessee, 2006.

Holloway, Joseph E. *New World African Press*. Baltimore, MD: Gateway Press Inc., 1983.

———. *The Slave Rebellion: African American Architecture: A Hidden Heritage*. Baltimore, MD: Gateway Press Inc., 1959.

Huguenot Society of Founders of Manakin in the Colony of Virginia. www.huguenotmanakin.org.

Hunter, Marker. "To the Sound of the Guns." www.markhunter.wordpress.com.

Kerby, Maude. *Midlothian: An American Village 1776–1976*. Midlothian, VA: Williams Job Printing, 1976.

Kimball, Gregg D. *American City, Southern Place: A Cultural History of Antebellum Richmond*. Athens: University of Georgia Press, 2003.

Knopp, Ken R. *Richmond Arsenal*. Richmond, VA: Self-published, 2008.

Kollatz, Harry, Jr. "The Gray Castle and the Mystery Basin." *Richmond Magazine*, 2011.

Lee, Richard M. *General Lee's City*. N.p.: EPM Publishing, 1987.

Library of Congress, Prints and Photographs.

Library of Richmond. *Powhatan Huguenots: French Huguenots to Virginia*. Richmond, VA: University of Richmond, n.d.

Library of Virginia. "Records of the Penitentiary." www.lva.virginia.gov.

————. Virginia Heritage Governor James Monroe Executive Papers, 1799–1802.

Lutz, Francis Earle. *Chesterfield: An Old Virginia County, 1607–1954.* Vol. 1. Chesterfield County, VA: Don Mills, Inc., 1954.

Lyle E. Browning and Associates. *Bellona Foundry.* Richmond, VA: J.K. Timmons and Associates, P.C., 1992.

Mallet, J.W., and O.E. Hunt. "The Ordnance of the Confederacy." University of Virginia.

————. "The Photographic History of the Civil War." University of Virginia.

Manakin Huguenot Society. "The Huguenot Society of the Founders of Manakin in the Colony of Virginia." www.huguenotmanakin.org.

Michel, Benjamin P. *The Richmond Armory History.* N.p.: n.d.

Moseley, Lucille C. *The Huguenot Houses in Powhatan and Chesterfield Counties.* Library of Congress. www.loc.org.

————. *Two Huguenot Houses at Keswick.* Huguenot Society of Founders of Manakin in the Colony of Virginia. www.huguenotmanakin.org.

"Murder at the Bellona Arsenal, 1828–1830." *Messenger*, August 2002. www.chesterfieldhistory.com.

National Register of Historic Places. Keswick. 1940.

————. Point of Forks Arenal. 1969.

————. Springhill Historic District. 2013.

O'Dell, Jeffery M. *Chesterfield County: Early Architecture and Historic Sites.* Chesterfield County, VA: Chesterfield County Planning Dept., 1983.

Palmer, Vera. *Gamble's Hill.* Richmond: Library of Virginia, 1962.

Poteet, David C. "The Armory Scandal: 1808–1809." *Virginia Cavalcade*, 1956.

————. *Arms for the Militia.* Richmond: Library of Virginia, 1966.

Powell Project. "Edmond J Eckel, 2015." www.powellproject.org.

Richmond Times-Dispatch Archives. Richmond, VA.

Scott, Mary Wingfield. "Old Richmond Neighborhood." William Byrd Press Inc., 1950.

Segar, Joseph, Esq. "Speech to the House of Delegates of Virginia." University of Richmond, 1861.

Singletary, Richard A. *The Spirits Know: Major John Clarke's Slave Source at Keswick Plantation.* Richmond: Virginia Commonwealth University, 1995.

Trabue Family Bible.

University of Virginia-Bellona. Pencil Drawing.

U.S. Department of the Interior. National Register of Historic Places. Keswick and Bellona Arsenal. Wanganui District Council Images.

Various Bellona articles. Chesterfield Historical Society of Virginia.

Virginia Commonwealth University Archives. www.digital.library.vcu.edu.

Virginia Historic Architectural Survey. Powhatan County. November 25, 1991. Traceries, 1606 Twentieth Street, N.W. Washington, D.C. 20001. *Keswick.*

Virginia Manufactory of Arms. American Society of Arms Collectors. Charlotte, NC, 2010.

Weaver, Bettie Woodson. *Midlothian: Highlights of Its History.* Chesterfield County, VA: Chesterfield County Public Schools, 1994.

Wilkes, Gerald P. *Virginia Division of Mineral Resources.* Charlottesville: University of Virginia, 1988.

"Women in Civil War Arsenals Project." *Richmond Examiner,* March 14, 1863.

Woodlief, Ann. *In River Times: The Way of the James Taming of the Falls.* Charlottesville, VA: VCU Archive, 1985.

Woodson, Bettie Woodson. *History and Geography of Chesterfield County, Virginia.* Chesterfield County, VA: Chesterfield County Public Schools, 1994.

Woodson, Frank S. "Bellona Arsenal, Hive of History." 1912.

———. *Chesterfield County Virginia: A History.* Midlothian, VA: Easterly Family, 1970.

Yates, Julie Trabue. *The Trabue Family in America 1700–1983.* Baltimore, MD: Gateway Press Inc., 1983.

Zehmer, John G. *The Church Hill: Old & Historic Districts.* Richmond, VA: Historic Richmond Foundation, 2011.

INDEX

A

antebellum period 11, 72, 90, 93, 94, 97, 104, 105, 109

B

Bellona Foundry 12, 35, 39, 40, 42, 43, 44, 45, 47, 51, 52, 54, 69, 70, 133, 134, 135, 136, 138, 142, 143
Brown's Island 58, 78, 80, 87, 125, 128

C

circular building 28, 30
coal 34, 35, 41, 45, 47, 56, 72, 74, 75, 88, 90, 140, 143
coke 34, 45, 49

Columbiads 43, 44, 47, 49, 130, 135
Confederate States Laboratory 125

D

Dover Mills 140

G

Gorgas 57, 130, 143, 161
Gray Castle 81

H

Harpers Ferry 34, 61, 62, 66, 131, 132, 155

J

James River 12, 16, 21, 22, 23, 26, 33, 34, 35, 38, 39, 40, 41, 42, 45, 49, 51, 52, 54, 55, 56, 59, 63, 66, 70, 80, 81, 83, 84, 87, 90, 94, 108, 116, 125, 128, 135, 139, 140, 142, 143, 152, 154, 157, 159, 164

L

Library Furnace 57

M

Mayo 90, 96, 98, 108, 116, 122, 150

N

Native American 25

P

penitentiary 26, 55, 59, 61, 63, 66, 83, 85, 87, 88, 146, 151
pig iron 54, 134, 135

R

Randolph 20, 35, 41, 76, 112, 114, 120, 122, 123, 145, 154, 159, 162, 164
Reed Pond 42, 52

Richmond 9, 11, 12, 20, 26, 32, 34, 35, 37, 38, 39, 41, 45, 47, 49, 55, 57, 58, 59, 60, 62, 63, 64, 65, 66, 69, 70, 78, 79, 81, 83, 84, 85, 87, 89, 90, 91, 92, 93, 94, 97, 98, 99, 100, 102, 103, 104, 106, 108, 109, 112, 113, 114, 115, 117, 119, 122, 125, 128, 130, 131, 132, 135, 137, 138, 140, 142, 143, 146, 147, 149, 150, 151, 153, 154, 155, 156, 158, 159, 160, 161, 162, 163, 164, 165
Richmond Hill 113, 116, 119
Richmond Penitentiary 80, 85, 162
Robinson 10, 140
Round Building 29

S

smokehouse 27, 28
Spring Creek 41, 52
St. John's Church 112

T

Trabue 12, 15, 16, 22, 23, 56, 69, 142, 143, 145, 146, 149, 150, 151, 153, 154, 155, 157
Tredegar 34, 41, 44, 45, 47, 48, 54, 57, 58, 66, 79, 81, 87, 89, 128, 130, 140, 143, 145, 146, 154, 155, 164
Turner 47, 75, 154

U

Union Hill 78, 90, 91, 92, 93, 102,
        105, 111

V

Virginia Armory 58, 81
Virginia Manufactory of Arms 26,
        34, 38, 55, 57, 58, 61, 62, 66,
        68, 128, 146, 150, 151, 155,
        156, 159, 161, 162
Virginia State Penitentiary 85

W

Westham Foundry 35, 36, 38, 59, 150
Wirt 5, 41, 42, 43, 69, 81, 145, 151

Y

yak 51

About the Author

Maurice Robinson is a native of Virginia; he worked for the RF&P Railroad in Virginia for twenty-one years. He was later transferred to Ponte Vedra Beach, Florida, where he lived and worked for fifteen years as an accountant with CSX Corporation. He retired in 2003, after working for thirty-five years. Robinson holds a bachelor's degree from Virginia Commonwealth University and has completed writing classes at the University of North Florida. With an interest in Florida's "First Coast" history, which he has already completed two books and one spiritual book about his miraculous recovery, Robinson is now attempting to write about a historical topic in Richmond and Chesterfield Counties about Richmond, Bellona and Keswick. He has resided for the last thirteen years in historic Midlothian, Virginia.

Also by Maurice Robinson:

Hidden History of Ponte Vedra. Charleston, SC: The History Press, 2012.

Life After Death Threatened; How Prayer Brought Back My Life. Bloomington, IN: WestBow Press, a Division of Thomas Nelson, 2012.

Ponte Vedra Beach: A History. Charleston, SC: The History Press, 2008.

Visit us at
www.historypress.com